Endors

"Wes Cantrell's book, From the Shop Floor to the Top Floor, describes the principles that have served Wes well in his journey from the bottom to the top. This is a real life story of the parable of the talents, where one man was entrusted with more because of how he used his current circumstances to serve others. We are treated to a first person experience of how God promotes those who are committed to serve where they are. It reminds us all that if we desire the next opportunity of service, we must ensure that we have been faithful in little. The good news is Wes continues to demonstrate that these principles work in all aspects of life, even after you've left the board room."

Sonny Perdue, Governor of Georgia

"Wes Cantrell is one of those living legends whose life firmly attests to the fact that there is room at the top, for the little guy with big vision, clear purpose and strong belief. In fact, regardless of your beginnings, you can finish on top and strong by following the profound life lessons penned by a man who has walked out every principle and step he proposes to you! If you weren't born with a silver spoon in your mouth and it's a long way from your floor to the top floor, this book is definitely for you! Rarely in life does one have the opportunity to rub shoulders with a man of great character, accomplishment and humility, let alone call him a friend but Wes Cantrell is all that and more. It's rare in life that we get to pull out the greatest success secrets of a man who has no other agenda but to pass on what he knows to you and I that we might discover and release the CEO Within! This book is a must read for every aspiring entrepreneur, executive and employee who knows deep down inside there is a CEO on the inside of them with a vision to make a difference. This is your chance to learn from a man who climbed the ladder of success and never forgot where he came from, nor lost sight of where he was going."

Michael Q. Pink, author of Rainforest Strategy, Selling Among Wolves and The Bible Incorporated and founder of the Rainforest Institute.

"When you meet Wes Cantrell, you instinctively want to pull him into a corner and begin mining for the large deposits of wisdom he clearly possesses. Now, through *Releasing the CEO Within,,* you too can learn from a proven leader how to achieve God's best for you and your work life."

> Dr. Richard Blackaby, co-author of *Experiencing God, Spiritual Leadership, God in the Marketplace."*

"Wes Cantrell does a wonderful job of translating the best business book of all-time, the Bible, into a roadmap for personal and professional success. His traditional advice is timeless and particularly helpful to those lower and middle level managers looking to move up in their organizations."

> Don Miller, President and CEO, Piedmont Office Realty Trust

"In *From the Shop Floor to the Top Floor*, Wes gives you the 'inside story' of his life in business. You will learn about his wonderful work in transforming his organization by focusing on the character and purpose of the business, and find out how you can do this too. You'll see how attitudes you've picked up along the way can work against your own future success and how these are often based on faulty ideas, what I've called in an earlier book *Fatal Illusions*. And you will receive great insight on how to build a personal foundation that can take you from wherever you are to wherever you dream you want to be.

I have known Wes for years and had the pleasure of co-authoring an earlier book with him. He is a man of great character, wisdom, and understanding. He brings to his work with others a solid mixture of excellent principles and hands-on experience. He has successfully mentored many people, and in this book will illustrate many ways to help you join that winning group. He is also a grand storyteller with a fine sense of humor, so you'll find this an enjoyable and entertaining read as well.

It's rare when someone with Wes Cantrell's great track record of success takes the time to share that with people like you and me. You will profit in many ways by reading this, a book that combines an enduring approach to work and leadership with ideas and examples that are as fresh as just-from-the-oven bread.

> James R. Lucas, President & CEO of Luman International, and co-author (with Wes) of *High-Performance Ethics: 10 Timeless Principles for Next-Generation Leadership* (www. highperformanceethics.com), and author of *The Passionate Organization, Passionate Lives & Leaders, Broaden the Vision and Narrow the Focus: Managing in a World of Paradox, Fatal Illusions,* and *Balance of Power*

Wes answers the question, "How did you start as a repairman and become CEO of the same company?" He answers in vivid detail with stories and illustrations from his 46 year career. Could this be done in today's environment? Wes says "yes" by obeying Biblical principles. I've known Wes for more than 20 years and have seen him at work and at play. His life and family all testify to the fact that these principles can take you to your top floor.

> David "Mac" McQuiston, CEO of the CEO Forum

Wes Cantrell is an authentic Christian executive who built a billion dollar business. This is his story about how he started at the bottom and rose to the top. He wanted to change Lanier from the inside out, focusing on a different purpose for the company. It's the story of the great American dream done God's way, which results in true contentment. A must read for every Christian businessman who wants to release the CEO within and find success from God's perspective.

> Bobby Mitchell, Chairman, Fellowship of Companies for Christ International.

Happy Father's Day

All my love,

[signature]

6/20/10

From the Shop Floor to the Top Floor

Releasing the CEO Within

Wes Cantrell

To Paul,

Blessings

Wes Cantrell

Prov 22:1

CROSSBOOKS
PUBLISHING

CrossBooks™
1663 Liberty Drive
Bloomington, IN 47403
www.crossbooks.com
Phone: 1-866-879-0502

First published by CrossBooks 12/21/2009

ISBN: 978-1-6150-7108-1 (sc)

Library of Congress Control Number: 2009912909

Some stories in the book were previously published in part in "High-Performance
Ethics," Tyndale House Publishers, 2007

All Scripture references are from the New King James Version unless otherwise noted.

About the Author Photo Credit: Dick Ruiz

Printed in the United States of America

Bloomington, Indiana
This book is printed on acid-free paper.

Dedication

With great love and appreciation, this book is dedicated to my wife of 53 years. As you read you will note that Bernadine has been at my side for over 44 of my 46 year business career. She has been my counselor, advisor, and confidante through all these years and she has helped me capture my thoughts in this book. She's a very expressive writer and you will experience her special touch as you read.

She has been a marvelous wife, mother and teacher. She has mentored many young women and seen the fruits of her labor of love in their lives as well as the lives of our children and grandchildren. She has demonstrated the true meaning of love by giving and serving others, particularly me! And at 72 years of age, she's still drop dead gorgeous, a true blessing of the Lord. Thank you, Bernadine, for all the great memories. I now fully understand the Scripture, "He who finds a wife finds a good thing, and obtains favor from the LORD." (Proverbs 18:22)

Acknowledgments

It has been a joy to write this book. I have viewed it as a ministry to anyone, but especially to men and women who work in the marketplace. It could not have been done without the advice, editing skills, and insight of my wife, Bernadine. She has been my partner throughout this adventure as she actually experienced firsthand many of the stories contained herein. Her advice and spiritual intuition are above any valuation known to man.

Our four children have blessed me by reading, editing, and advising. They walked through many of these career years with me. I'm grateful for their Godly lives.

Through the years I have been blessed with many pastors, teachers, and friends who have had a major impact on my life and consequently on this book. One of my best friends and advisors was Larry Burkett. His *Business by the Book* greatly impacted my life, and you see that reflected in my writing. Years ago I called Larry and confessed that I had plagiarized some of his book in my writing. He said, "Don't worry about it, Wes; I plagiarized it all from the Bible."

The teaching of Mike Gilchrist, Bill Gothard, Carroll Phillips, Charles Stanley, T. P. Johnston, and Johnny Hunt and the writing of Chris Tiegreen and Oswald Chambers have all had a major impact on my life and my writing. I am grateful to each of them.

The best example for my life was that of my father, James Wesley Cantrell. He was a country preacher and actually practiced what he preached—and more. His advice was excellent and his example was without question. Through many hard times, his faith never wavered.

Foreword

There must be a major reason for feeling good about writing an introduction to a book. I believe that it is of utmost importance that integrity be maintained and the truth be shared. With that being said, excitement is probably the understatement of the year about this new book. It is a joy to read the pages of a book written by a man who understands his position as it relates to his relationship with Almighty God that has been developed through the Lord Jesus Christ. Wes realizes that wherever God positions you in life becomes your ministry platform. He understands God's place in his heart as it relates to the marketplace.

If a man desires to be a good leader, he must be one who realizes that God has placed him here to serve; therefore, he must also be a follower. Wes Cantrell exemplifies the type characteristics of a leader that makes it a joy to follow. He understands God's principles and defines well what it takes to become a leader in this volume. It is one thing to think about what you would do if God chose to trust you with affluence, and it is another thing to have experienced it and passed the test. It is important to understand how much is enough and God's purpose for the wealth that He has given you. I love to pick up a book that challenges me to be a man of excellence as it pertains to every area of my life. You will find that this book will help you in building a life that helps others to succeed. Wes is encouraging you to build with the best. In order to become the person and the leader that you desire to be, there are places you must go and there are places that you must leave. Again, you will be helped as you read of the things that must be removed in order to get to the place you desire to be. There must be the relinquishing before there can be the apprehending. I feel that by the time you finish this book, and place it in the hands of someone else · that you care deeply for, you will resolve within your heart, with clear discrimination, the type leader that you desire to be and the steps that it will take to be that man or woman.

Finally, one of the major encouragements of this book is realizing that in order to become the leader that you desire to be, there is one group you never leave behind, namely, your family. What an incredible encouragement you will receive as you learn how to unify your job and your family. Often a person asks, "Why am I here, what am I here for, and where am I going?" I trust that by the time you close this volume you will have found God's purpose for your life and determined that nothing will deter you from His purpose for your journey.

Again, Wes Cantrell, in the years that I have been privileged to know him personally, has emulated the principles that he writes about. These are personal matters. Be blessed, and pass it on.

Dr. Johnny M. Hunt
President of the Southern Baptist Convention
Pastor, First Baptist Church, Woodstock

Contents

Introduction

"You'll never make it!" Those words still resound in my memory because they were spoken by my boss. This was especially discouraging because I had no idea what the Lord had planned for me, no idea that He had designed a future that I could never have imagined. At that time I didn't know that the Lord was even interested in my business career. Although I was a committed Christian and was active in church, I had not connected my vocation to His plan.

My personal mission in writing this book is to facilitate the release of your "CEO within." That phrase holds much promise. Certainly not everyone will be a CEO of a big company, but everyone is called by God to some kind of occupation. Everyone is CEO of something, whether it's your family or your own life.

Recently we observed a profound example of this concept. My wife and I were visiting a couple, the Armisteads, who were prospects for our Bible class. Todd proudly encouraged his wife, Staci, to show her business card to me. Carefully I inspected the card advertising Armistead & Associates, underscored with the slogan: "We bring good things to life." Staci was the Vice President for a *most* important business. She was a stay-at-home mom. Some would refer to Staci as "only a housewife." But she had a totally different perspective of her vocation.

The good news is that God has plans for you and that includes your vocation. When you understand God's plan and invite Him to work in your life, there is great release of His Spirit and your progress will be accelerated. Also, you will experience tremendous enjoyment in your work.

Ephesians 2:10 tells us, "We are His workmanship, created in Christ Jesus for good works, which God prepared beforehand that we should walk in them." We were created for good works! It's quite clear that God has a plan that He created in advance for us to follow. The major thrust of this book is discovering and walking in His plan and not our own?

Your fundamental beliefs about God, success, and wealth are the basis of true and lasting achievement. When these are established in your thinking by seeing from God's perspective, you will realize the purpose for which you were created. True success from the Lord's perspective is incredibly different from that of the world system, and it ushers contentment into life.

I am frequently asked how I was able to rise from the position of repairman to CEO. I'm also asked if this is still possible in today's business climate. My answer is yes, it is still possible because fundamental principles do not change.

A few years ago, Bernadine and I were in Washington attending a convention. When we entered the elevator in the Ritz Carlton and pressed the button, nothing happened. Then I realized that you must insert your room key in the slot in order to move up. The principle crystallized in my mind—you must have the key to move up. Seven keys are detailed in this book that will facilitate your progress in any vocation.

Through application of these principles, you will experience a new enthusiasm and purpose in your life. Whatever your present role, you can have a new sense of direction and power. My prayer is that the Lord will bless you richly as you share part of my life and learn from my experiences and insights.

Chapter One

The Basis of Release

God in the market place

Lanier had grown rapidly. We were entering a new business with an exciting and revolutionary product. We were soon to be spun off from our parent company and would be listed on the New York Stock Exchange. Adding to the excitement, we had just signed well known golfer Arnold Palmer as our corporate sponsor. Recently I had been promoted and was now Vice President and National Sales Manager.

These events were the prelude to one of the most surprising and exhilarating events of my career. I was invited to attend a meeting to honor Sartain Lanier, one of the founders of the company. My boss asked me to prepare an appropriate plaque and presentation for Mr. Lanier. I was delighted to do so because of my long-standing admiration for this man whom I considered a financial wizard.

We had assembled in a private meeting room of a lovely Atlanta hotel when my wife walked into the room with a big smile on her face. I wasn't expecting her and the surprise of her presence shook me with anticipation. My racing pulse struggled to keep pace with my thoughts: "What is going on? This is not what I was prepared for." Somehow I knew whatever was happening was going to be good!

Gene Milner, Chairman of the Board stood to welcome everyone. He promptly announced that I had been elected president of the company by the Board of Directors. I held my churning emotions in check; I showed a cool exterior, but inside my imagination was busy with thoughts of the future. A far-fetched notion had become a reality. Even though I had been promoted several times, the idea of being made president seemed to be against all odds. At that time Lanier was a family owned company. I thought the job would most likely go to a member of the family.

Since I had started my career as a repairman, often I was asked, "When did you make being president your goal?" My answer seems to surprise people. I didn't think being president was a likely possibility for me. I had simply focused on performing my present job with excellence. As a repairman, I had focused on satisfying every customer. As a salesman I had focused on delivering more than promised to each customer. As a manager I had focused on developing people. In each case I had recognized that productivity was a requirement. All of this was driven by my evolving concept of success, which was rooted in understanding how God was involved in my work.

So who releases the "CEO within"? When I became president, I knew that it was not the work of man; the Lord was orchestrating His plan. The execution of His plan was based on my faith and obedience.

The History of Work

Our labor is the basis of support for all institutions established by God. Throughout the Bible, almost everyone is identified by his or her vocation. The first mention of Adam's children, Cain and Abel, pertains to their vocations: Abel was a shepherd and Cain was a farmer. Other vocations mentioned in Scripture include lawyer, physician, carpenter, silversmith, tax collector, fisherman, soldier, sailor, merchant, moneychanger, priest, governor, and more.

Work is an important part of God's design for man. God has always called working people. Moses was a shepherd whom God called to lead His people, and David tended his father's sheep before being called to rule over Israel. Four fishermen were invited to become fishers of men. Paul was a tentmaker who used his trade to support his ministry. Lydia was a seller of purple. Jesus was a carpenter. We were created for work, and our vocations provide the means to support our families as well as other institutions God has established.

Work Supports the Family

From the time of creation it has been God's plan for man to work. Although the first family had the ideal situation, Adam and Eve disobeyed God. One of the repercussions of disobedience was that man's established work became much more difficult. Adam's vocation changed from supervising a beautiful garden to tilling the rocky soil of a weedy, thorn-infested field. This is the first example in history that disobedience leads to a "rocky path."

One purpose of work is to support the family. The Bible states the imperative of supporting your family simply and emphatically: "If anyone does not provide for his relatives, and especially for members of his immediate family, he has denied the faith and is worse than an unbeliever." (I Timothy 5:8)

Work Supports the Government

The Lord set forth principles of government soon after man began to populate the earth. The nation of Israel was ruled by a God-appointed leader and a system of laws. The primary function of government was to protect its citizens; the citizens were to support the government.

When Moses was leading the children of Israel, he set up a system of judges to decide civil issues and settle disputes. God gave the Ten Commandments as the basis for the legal system. This became the foundation for the "rule of law" and was the cornerstone for governing all relationships—family, government, church, and business. Taxation was the method of support for government.

Joseph established a system of taxation when he was leading the government of Egypt. The Lord had revealed to him that a famine was coming in seven years. He set aside one-fifth of all harvested grain to be contributed to the government and stored (Genesis 41:34). This was a 20-percent "flat tax" on all grain produced and was not progressive. The purpose of Joseph's plan was for the protection of all citizens—food for the famine.

When Rehoboam became king of Israel, he gave his attention quickly to taxation. One of his first acts was to visit with the old men of his father Solomon's reign and hear their advice. They suggested that he relieve the burden (taxes) imposed on the people, as it was too heavy. Then Rehoboam met with the young men he grew up with and asked their advice. They recommended raising taxes and treating the old men harshly, thereby establishing his leadership and authority in the kingdom. Rehoboam did a foolish thing and followed the advice of his peers. This resulted in the division of the kingdom, and his tax collector was stoned to death (II Chronicles 10:4-18). People have always reacted strongly to taxation, yet taxes are the means of support for the government. Paying taxes is part of God's plan.

Three of the four Gospels tell the story of Jesus' response to questions about paying taxes to the hated Roman government. As He held a coin in His hand before the group, He inquired, "Whose image and title do you see on this coin?" They answered, "Caesar's." Then Jesus said, "Give to Caesar what is Caesar's and to God what is God's." (Mark 12:17 NIV)

Biblical instruction is clear; we are to pay our taxes: "Pay your taxes, too, for these same reasons. For government workers need to be paid. They are serving God in what they do." (Romans 13:6 NLT)

Work Supports the Church

When Cain and Abel brought their offerings to the Lord, we have our first clear picture of giving as an act of worship. Abram gave one-tenth of all the goods he had recovered from his enemies to Melchizedek, a priest of God (Genesis 14). This is the first mention of the tithe, or 10 percent, given for the support of God's work. Throughout the Old Testament, the tenth (tithe) is mentioned many times. It was intended to support the priests and Levites, to maintain the temple, and for the poor, particularly widows and orphans. The priests and Levites were to tithe their income as well even though it came from the tithes of others.

The Lord has given a marvelous promise of blessing to those who tithe: "'Bring all the tithes into the storehouse, that there may be food in My house, and try Me now in this, says the LORD of hosts, If I will not open for you the windows of heaven and pour out such blessing that there will not be room enough to receive it." (Malachi 3:10)

At the time of Jesus' ascension, He outlined the mission of the New Testament church that was being established. He commissioned Christians to go into the entire world, evangelizing and teaching the commands of Christ. (Matthew 28:19-20) If the church is to follow the command of Jesus, financial support is necessary. Scripture instructs the Christian to give based on what we have received: "We are to give as freely as we have received." (Matthew 10:8) We should also give regularly: "On the first day of every week, each of you is to put something aside and store it up, as he may prosper, so that there will be no collecting when I come." (1 Corinthians 16:2 ESV)

We should give cheerfully and generously to the local church. The purpose of giving is to support pastors and missionaries, give to the poor, take care of widows and orphans, and support the fulfillment of His commission. The Lord loves a cheerful giver: "Let each one give as he purposes in his heart, not grudgingly or of necessity; for God loves a cheerful giver." (II Corinthians 9:7)

The purpose of my work was clarified with the growing knowledge of God's plan to support the institutions He established. **There is no way to separate our walk from our work.** We are to glorify Him in all we do. (I Corinthians 10:31) He desires to reveal Himself in the context of our work. In the business world, it is His plan to infiltrate the marketplace. The Lord wants to use us in our work, as in all aspects of our lives. He has strategically set you in your vocation, and He gives instructions for your conduct in the marketplace. Behavior on the job is simply an extension of our personal behavior in all of life. This is fundamental to releasing your CEO within.

Marketplace Behavior

Christians should distinguish themselves with exemplary behavior. Those desired behaviors are given in this Scripture and several others: "Servants, obey in all things your masters according to the flesh, not with eyeservice, as men-pleasers, but in sincerity of heart, fearing God. And whatever you do, do it heartily, as to the Lord and not to men, knowing that from the Lord you will receive the reward of the inheritance; for you serve the Lord Christ. But he who does wrong will be repaid for what he has done, and there is no partiality." (Colossians 3:21-25 KJV)

Obey your Leaders

The term "servants" as used in these verses accurately translates to what we know in today's culture as "employees." Obeying our leaders speaks directly to our on-the-job attitude as we do our work "as to the Lord and not to men." The word "eye service" in this passage indicates a slothful, lazy attitude or being a people pleaser. Such a person might work hard under surveillance but slack off when no one is watching.

Source of Promotion

I had thought it unlikely I would become president of my company. The question frequently came to my mind, "Why me?" In my Bible study one day, Psalm 75 captured my attention. I could hardly believe what I read. God uses the authorities He appoints in our lives to direct our paths—even if they aren't aware of it.

"I said to the arrogant *and* boastful, Deal not arrogantly [do not boast]: and to the wicked, Lift not up the horn [of personal aggrandizement]. Lift not your [aggressive] horn on high, speak not with a stiff neck *and* insolent arrogance. For not from the east nor from the west or from the south comes promotion *and* lifting up. But God is the Judge! He puts down one and lifts up another." (Psalm 75:4-7 AMP)

The surprising news was that all promotion originates with the Lord. It doesn't come from others, but is His activity. Our part is spelled out—don't be self-promoting or "toot your own horn," but simply trust Him. I had observed many "horn blowers" in the corporate world. That attribute is repulsive and I wanted to stay on guard against it. We are told not to exalt ourselves: In Luke 14:11 "For whoever exalts himself will be humbled, and he who humbles himself will be exalted."

This Scripture demonstrates how He works in our lives—in ways we never could have imagined: "Now to Him Who, by (in consequence of) the [action of His] power that is at work within us, is able to [carry out His purpose and] do super abundantly, far over and above all that we [dare] ask or think [infinitely beyond our highest prayers, desires, thoughts, hopes, or dreams]." (Ephesians 3:20 AMP)

Tremendous relief and contentment are found in trusting this profound truth: Our promotion is a part of His plan. Energy and enthusiasm for our work surge when we acknowledge we are working for the Lord. This is Him at work in us. There is an entirely new dimension of genuine pleasure in our work. Concern for promotion no longer drains us of energy. It also helps eliminate the ego that is inflated by promotion.

The "ego attack" that sometimes accompanies promotion was best illustrated by a man I knew quite well. His first act when he became CEO of a company was to build a covered parking garage for his

Mercedes 500SL. There were no other covered parking places—only his! Gene, my boss for many years had this part right. He didn't believe in reserved parking places for anyone. He always said, "If you are that important, you should get there first."

Develop Humility

About three weeks after I initially started to work at Lanier as a technical trainee, I was told to go to the basement and clean the owner's fishing tackle. His boat had sunk and the tackle box was in dreadful condition. There was mud, seaweed, and a foul-smelling odor in that box. It was especially demeaning to be asked to do such a task. I went to the basement grumbling inside. After all, I had graduated at the top of my class and I was too good and too well educated to be doing this kind of work!

As I thought about this unpleasant job, it occurred to me that the owner of the company, the man whose signature was on my check, had asked me to do something. In spite of my earlier reluctant thoughts, I made a sound decision. Not only would I do what had been requested, I would do it thoroughly and exceptionally well! Carefully, I removed everything from the box. Every lure was meticulously polished and shining before I placed them back into the clean tackle box. I felt a great sense of satisfaction not only for doing a good job, but also from knowing I had made the right decision. Although I did not understand at the time, this experience is now etched in my mind as a personal example of "working as to the Lord."

In hindsight, I know this experience was a test. The owner understood the principle of learning and obedience. He had likely noticed my pride. Where there is pride, there can be no learning and development, and Mr. Lanier knew it. If someone thinks they already know everything, they cannot learn since there is no admitted need for growth. By breaking down my pride, he discovered early in my career that I would obey and humble myself to do what was required. James 4:6 states, "God resists the proud, but gives grace to the humble."

When you see a job that needs to be done, do it regardless of your rank or position. Go beyond the call of duty. Your doing whatever is at hand is a wonderful demonstration of servant leadership to those who

7

might be watching. Stepping up to bat, regardless of your position, is an outstanding leadership example.

Walk with Integrity

The underpinning behavior that glorifies the Lord in our work is integrity. The Merriam-Webster dictionary defines *integrity* as "firm adherence to a code of especially moral or artistic values." The Bible defines integrity through the life of Daniel. This code of behavior cannot be derived from secular practices, but rather from God's instructions. Daniel embraced God's principles in his heart. No fault could be found in his behavior. (Daniel 6:5) The charges brought against him were actually based on his integrity.

The Bible speaks of the results of integrity, or a lack of it: "The integrity of the upright guides them, but the perversity of the unfaithful will destroy them." (Proverbs 11:3) Integrity is a quality that permeates every aspect of a person's life. On-the-job behavior and attitudes give an outward picture of your integrity. A Christian should work diligently—there is no room for laziness. Many times dishonesty is the result of slothfulness. The lazy person is always looking for an easy way to get money, a way to get rich quick. When you work diligently, it will be noticed: "Do you see a man who excels in his work? He will stand before kings; He will not stand before unknown men." (Proverbs 22:29) Others observe your integrity through your behavior, but its root is in the heart.

Who pays you?

Compensation is one of the most heated subjects relating to our work. Once we understand that we are working for the Lord, we also know that it is the Lord who pays us. We receive our rewards both now as income and in eternity in His presence. When I adopted the attitude of doing my work for the Lord, it radically changed my approach to compensation negotiations. In fact, I placed no emphasis on negotiation. Instead I trusted the Lord to work through my leaders to pay the amount He desired for me.

Maintain good relationships

Conflict between employees consumes lots of business energy. Wrongdoing does happen at work, and at times you may bear the brunt of misconduct on the part of someone else. You may be falsely accused. Always speak the truth clearly and know that the Lord will deal with the problems in due season. When conflict is being resolved, some will say what they think the boss wants to hear rather than the absolute truth. We must be truthful, always providing accurate information. It is tempting to seek revenge and begin an evil-for-evil cycle. A vengeful, defensive reaction is natural (as opposed to spiritual) and wrong. Scripture tells us, "Never pay back evil for evil to anyone. Do things in such a way that everyone can see you are honorable . . . . Dear friends, never avenge yourselves. Leave that to God. For it is written, I will take vengeance; I will repay those who deserve it, says the Lord." (Romans 12:17, 19 NLT)

Honesty is required

The proper use of our time on the job is vitally significant. We must not misuse the time paid for by the employer by being late, talking on the phone, or surfing the Web for personal reasons. Christians should always give more than expected, show up earlier, and stay later. Excellence—doing our best in every aspect of our work should be our clarion call. There should be no hint of wrongdoing when our behavior is observed or examined. (I Thessalonians 5:22)

Honesty is not an optional business practice; it's a requirement. Most employees will face business situations where there are opportunities to cut corners, cheat, steal, or misrepresent the facts for personal advantage. The book of Proverbs mentions weights and measures repeatedly. For example, "Dishonest scales are an abomination to the LORD, but a just weight is His delight." (Proverbs 11:1) This method of measurement was used in Biblical times for buying and selling goods such as grain. Some merchants used one set of weights for the wealthy customers and another for the poor. The wealthy customer had his own weights at home and would double-check the merchant, so fear of discovery kept him honest. Not so for the poor customers. God instructed His people: "You shall not have in your house differing measures, a large and a small." (Deuteronomy 25:14) Honesty is to be extended to everyone at all times; fear of discovery is not the Christian's guideline. The Bible promises, "He who hates unjust gain will prolong his days." (Proverbs 28:16 ESV) Simply stated, the Lord hates cheating but He delights in honesty, and His followers will be healthier and live longer as an added benefit!

The U.S. Department of Commerce estimates for employee theft range from $10 to $150 billion annually. Obviously, temptation is always present. Let us Christians be meticulously honest in caring for our employer's property. We must be on guard even against casual misuse.

When I became president of Lanier, I used many company supplies for personal projects. Paper clips, transparencies, copy paper, ballpoint pens, marking pens, and many other office supply items were needed for our projects at home. The mail room often mailed packages for me. This was a major convenience. I asked my administrative assistant to keep a log of all such expenses. To my surprise, my annual reimbursement to the company totaled $600 to $1,000. You can be sure that every employee was watching my behavior. It was good to set a proper example, but it was even better to know I was being honest where others could not see—in my heart. To counter the great temptation to cheat, effective leadership in the workplace is a tremendous need. Be the contagious honest example in every facet of attitude and behavior.

Protect Customers

The customer should get everything he has paid for and more, providing a little more than expected. In Louisiana, the Cajuns call that *lagniappe*—a little something extra for the customer. What a great rule for satisfied customers and what a great attitude in an employee!

In the sales process, unsupported claims are sometimes made, customer testimonies are exaggerated, and incentives are provided to charge as much as the traffic will bear. Some businesses offer the sales rep half of everything they get above the target price, a risky and unfair policy. There are legitimate reasons for price differences, which include volume discounts, cash discounts, class discounts (for example, senior citizen discounts), and meeting competitive prices. With few exceptions, prices should be the same for everyone.

One customer told me that she continued to buy from us because our sales rep never lied to her. Apparently, others were careless and had more than one version of the facts. Through customer surveys, we learned the main reason we were successful in the face of formidable competition was that customers trusted our representatives. Creating an attitude of trust with customers by keeping your word and being meticulously honest is Biblical, but it is also good for business!

The Japanese business culture appears to be based on Christian values. Less than 3 percent of the people in Japan are Christians; yet, as a basic practice, Japanese business men keep their word. Why do they work so diligently to provide what is needed for our customers? Why are they so easy to deal with? The answer is simple—they have learned that it's good for business and Japan is ALL about business. They have adopted Christian values because they produce the best results in business relationships.

Make a profit

Some people think that making a profit is wrong, and this has always puzzled me. Without the profit motive, productivity suffers. Who would go to the trouble to plant a crop if there was no hope of reaping more than you sowed? The profit motive works. We give from the increase. Without a profit, the business owner would have nothing to give to the Lord's work. "In all labor there is profit, but idle chatter leads only to poverty." *(*Proverbs 14:23)

Be Trustworthy

Loyalty is extremely important. We should be loyal to our employer and to our leaders. If we realize that we cannot remain loyal; it's time to evaluate. Is the company dishonest? Is my boss dishonest? Should I consider leaving? Is my ambition destructive? Do I have a secret agenda that prevents me from being loyal? Am I being manipulative, causing my leader to react? After completing this self-examination, your decision must be, "If I remain, I must be loyal. Otherwise, I should leave." Proverbs 27:18 speaks to the benefits of loyalty: "As workers who tend a fig tree are allowed to eat its fruit, so workers who protect their employer's interests **[loyalty]** will be rewarded." (Proverbs 27:18 NLT, explanation added)

Calling the Ordinary

It is striking that none of Jesus' disciples were theologians or priests. They were ordinary workers or businessmen, mostly rough, uneducated men whose lives were transformed. The Lord validated weak and imperfect people by giving them value through their relationship with Him. Now, just as in Biblical times, the Lord sends His weak and imperfect people into the marketplace as His ministers. Knowing that you are about His business in your designated job will result in contentment and new meaning in your work. Recognizing the calling the Lord had placed on my life as His minister in the marketplace brought a whole new perspective to my vocation. I placed new significance on everything I did on the job each day.

In Luke 10, Jesus refers to the 72 He sends out as "workers" or "laborers." He says, "The harvest truly is great, but the laborers are few; therefore pray the Lord of the harvest to send out laborers into His harvest." (Luke 10:2) And that is the way we should view ourselves—as His workers. He describes them as lambs among wolves, His servants in the marketplace (Luke 10:1-3). We are to serve others and use our voices and lives to show Him to the world around us. Availability to be used by Him on the job sheds a whole new light on the workplace. When we experience how God uses us in our work through our relationships, there is pleasure and an increased level of energy. Our productivity soars!

Get in on what He's up to

In the Old Testament account of the children of Israel, many of their kings failed. The most-repeated phrase describing those failed kings is, "They consulted not the LORD." This gives us the caution—we should consult the Lord in all things. There is no question that prayer (consulting Him) is a powerful weapon. As we get in on His plans, we can count on His results.

One of our employees who had previously worked for a competitor told me an interesting story. In his previous position he had heard me described as "religious," and had heard, "He even prays about business situations and everyone knows it, how ridiculous!" Obviously it was not meant as a compliment. I suggested that he send a message to the competitor: "Your concern should not be that he prays—but that his prayers are being answered!"

Private prayer is an ongoing practice of mine, but it was keenly developed during many of my business challenges. For example, in the seventies, the country was in a major recession. Everything was tight, prices were increasing, and most businesses were discouraged and losing ground. Layoffs, price hikes, and cutbacks were the normal practices of the day. Interest rates, unemployment, and inflation were at all-time highs. In our business, we saw this economic condition as an opportunity.

At this time, Lanier had several new products ready for market. Since our competitors were retreating, we decided to charge ahead aggressively. To our advantage, sales reps were easier to hire because of the high unemployment throughout the country. We advertised, introduced new products, hired sales reps, and had a great year. It was quite an unusual accomplishment in view of the recession, and the press noted our success.

Sales and Marketing Management Magazine asked for an interview. Their primary question was, "Why is your company having such great results when all your competitors are struggling?" The interview resulted in an article entitled, "A Funny Thing Happened on the Way to the Recession!" As a result, I was asked to speak to the Sales and Marketing Executives Club in New York City at the Waldorf Astoria. I visualized myself speaking to a large group of New York big shots. For a country boy with a southern accent and limited experience in the "big city," it was a terrifying thought.

As I prepared for this presentation, fervent prayer was my solace. Prayerful preparation was my confidence as I faced this challenge. I worked diligently on my talk and had it down pat before that fateful morning. I went to the big city as His representative. When I was introduced, I stood with a sense of confidence, not in myself, but in Him and His presence in my life. The speech was a big hit.

Later I was asked to give the same talk in Los Angeles and San Francisco—two more big-city challenges. These were thrilling opportunities. I continually remembered, "God has not given us a spirit of fear, but of power and of love, and of a sound mind." (II Timothy 1:7) The thought of that promise and reliance upon the Promise Giver gave me great confidence to enter the marketplace as His representative.

As you determine the primary focus of your life, remember that ministry comes after your relationship with the Lord and the priority of your family. Indeed, your vocation is a priority as well. Most people will spend more time on the job than in any other activity in their lives. Work is a ministry. Just as surely as God calls missionaries and preachers, He calls us all to be laborers (ministers) in our work.

"A dairy maid can milk cows to the glory of God."
—*Martin Luther*

The Lord is the Originator of all good ideas and creativity comes from Him. He knows all the answers to all of our questions and He will let you in on the information if you simply relinquish the control to Him rather than depending upon yourself. Proverbs 3:5-6: "Trust in the LORD with all your heart and lean not on your own understanding; in all your ways acknowledge him and he will make your paths straight." (NIV)

When His purpose becomes our purpose, our eyes open to a whole new world during the time that we are on the job. Whether managing a service station, working as a plumber, cleaning a house, teaching in a classroom, sorting in the mail room, or chairing a meeting in the boardroom, your workplace is a "field white unto harvest." It is a place to be esteemed, to be enjoyed, and to achieve personal satisfaction of a job well done, because the Lord has placed you there. Proverbs 16:3 promises, "Commit your works to the LORD, and your thoughts will be established." The Lord takes great pleasure in our work when we honor Him. There were many miracles I experienced at the Lord's hand: becoming president against all odds, overwhelming success in my first management assignment, acquisitions that simply dropped into our laps, becoming CEO, becoming a member of the Horatio Alger Association, receiving an honorary doctorate from Southern Polytechnic State University—all orchestrated by the Lord. As I recall these cherished BIG events, I praise my Lord, who was working in the SMALL details as well. I boast only in Him whom I desire to glorify.

Eric Liddell said it best in the movie *Chariots of Fire*: "God made me for a purpose, but He also made me fast. And when I run I feel His pleasure." May you feel His pleasure as He releases your CEO within!

Chapter Two

The Key of Responding

Becoming a great follower

The sales meeting was held at the Dinkler Plaza Hotel in downtown Atlanta. All the top sales reps attended and there were rousing presentations. It was a remarkably exciting atmosphere. As a young and inexperienced salesman, I was learning how the pros did it.

In the course of the meeting, my boss called me aside and told me we were going to lunch—somewhere else. This was a signal that there was to be an intentional discussion. He was an intimidating presence and everyone was cautious about disagreeing with him. Over lunch, Gene told me that I might have an extremely bright future with the company, moving up from my sales position in Augusta, Georgia, except for one hindrance. "I have heard that you won't take a drink," he said. He further explained that drinking is a big part of how business is done and without drinking at least a social drink, I would never make it. His concluding remark became etched in my memory: "I would be insulted if you invited me to your home and did not offer me a drink!"

As a young boy, I made a pledge to the Lord through the leadership of a caring Sunday school teacher. There were three elements of the pledge I signed. I promised to abstain from the use of tobacco, to abstain from alcohol, and to use my voice to praise the Lord. Proudly, my parents displayed the framed document in our home. Even though earlier in life I strayed from this commitment, I had never forgotten it! Although the print on the paper had faded with age, the memory of the desire of the young boy's heart became incredibly important. As my dear Sunday school teacher had offered me a choice, now Gene was presenting another choice.

As Gene studied me intently and waited for my response, I carefully weighed the importance of my answer. Would I compromise my earlier commitment in order to succeed in business? After a few moments, I replied, "I guess I'll just have to be your top salesman in Augusta for the rest of my career."

In every job, there is opportunity to respond to your leaders. There are many different personalities that will be encountered—you may eventually work for a certified tyrant. My boss of 30 years would certainly fit into that category. He was mean, angry, and cantankerous. In our business journey together, I discovered a spiritual principle that allowed me to work with him effectively.

Release depends significantly on learning to respond correctly to every leader. In my career, I worked with nine bosses. They were all different and I learned from each one. Some folks have a bad attitude toward all authority. They hate the word "boss" and they wouldn't consider the word "obey." Others change jobs to find a more acceptable boss, but then they gain the reputation of being a job hopper—an employee who can't get along with any boss. With the attitude of trying to escape authority, they will never realize their full potential. Responding properly to all authority is a **key** requirement for release of your CEO within.

Authority plays a major role in receiving direction from God. Each authority organization which God planned and originated—the family, government, the church and business can and will be used to afford us direction as we seek His best in our decision-making process. In the family, there is an authority structure. Children are commanded to obey their parents and wives to submit to their husbands. This is God's order, establishing a clear line of authority and maintaining order, discipline and effectiveness in each family (Ephesians 5:22-6:2).

God also established government and appointed our authorities, and they are His ministers to us. We are commanded to obey governmental authorities. God has appointed all authority. We are to obey our leaders in order to have a clear conscience and for our protection (Romans 13:1-5).

In the church we are also to obey our spiritual leaders and submit to their authority. They have been appointed by the Lord to keep watch over our souls. At their level of responsibility, they will give an account for everything they do. Let them do their job freely and with joy. Do not complain because that is of no advantage (Hebrews 13:7).

On the job we are told to obey our leaders and not to answer back. The Lord has placed us in specific situations; therefore we have an authority over us in our vocation. In our work, being submissive is ultimately an act of service to God and not man (Colossians 3:22).

We are to obey those placed over us. In your family, you did not choose your parents—but in each of the other structures, you have a choice. You choose where to live, what church to attend, and where you work. With those three choices, you have also chosen authority structures. When we move away from disliked, disagreeable, and difficult authorities we miss a primary source of God's guidance. One of God's principal means of providing direction in life is through our authorities.

When I applied for my job with Lanier, this question appeared on the application form: "Would you like to go into business for yourself?" This was an interesting question designed to expose the applicant's desire to be his or her own boss. A "yes" answer requires further discussion to determine the applicant's intent. Is this a sign of independence from someone who wants to be their own boss because they dislike the very idea of authority? Or is this someone with a strong entrepreneurial spirit looking for a vocation where they can freely exercise their talent? Skillful questioning would expose the motive.

After I had been employed for about three months at Lanier, the owner of the business called me to his office and asked me, "Cantrell, how soon can you be in Baton Rouge, Louisiana?" He wasn't talking about a business trip. He meant re-location on a permanent basis. Always in awe of Mr. Lanier and his strong personality, and not knowing the distance to Baton Rouge, I responded with my first thought: "How about first thing tomorrow?" He smiled and suggested that I take a few days to get things in order.

The truth was, I was shocked and really didn't want to leave Atlanta. My present situation was quite comfortable. I was living with my parents, and my mother washed my clothes and cooked for me. I had a girlfriend and a new car. Things were going quite well, and I saw no reason to upset all this by relocating. Another interesting aspect was the fact that I had an offer from IBM for a job that would be available in a few weeks. I was entertaining the thought of quitting my job at Lanier and staying in Atlanta.

That evening, I told my father what had happened. My father was a man of few words; when he spoke, I listened. Recalling our conversations is easy and pleasant. Although his words were few— they were always wise. He said, "Son, if you ever want to amount to anything, you'll need to go where that company sends you." With no further consideration, I immediately made plans to leave for Baton Rouge.

In late September, Baton Rouge is very hot—I'd never been in a climate quite like it! Few establishments had air conditioning. Upon arrival, I moved into a boarding house and quickly began to make friends.

On October 31, a friend invited me to walk downtown to the drugstore. That night I met a lovely Louisiana girl. It was her 18th birthday and she was the real deal. She was the girl of my dreams! One year plus a few months later we were married. We are still happily married today.

In hindsight, I know that my life would have been quite different had I not listened to my two authorities about that particular move to Louisiana—one at work and one at home. I am confident that the Lord provided His divine guidance through these two individuals. I'm sure my father thought it was time I moved out of the house, and he probably was concerned about my dating situation. Whatever his reason or motive, he provided firm direction and I heeded it. The result was 53 years of happy marriage with 4 children, 22 grandchildren, and the additional blessings of great-grandchildren. Even though I did not realize God's divine guidance at the time, I am so grateful that He led me through the authorities He had established in my family and in my workplace.

A key to responding to any and all authorities is to realize that the Lord has placed them in your life for a purpose. When we resist, we delay the shaping, sculpting, and developing of the qualities the Lord desires in our lives.

Rather than running from an unethical boss, carefully consider confronting him or her. Recognize the possible consequences. You are putting your neck on the block, and there is the possibility that you could lose your job. Ask the Lord for wisdom and discernment to understand the authority figure's goals. Prayer and total dependence upon the Lord, along with careful thought and planning are your responsibility. Unethical behavior is most likely a shortcut. Present your creative idea of achieving your authority's goals but with ethical behavior. Be prepared, they may not accept your plan!

You will have the privilege of responding to several different styles of leadership during your career. There is no question that a difficult boss can make a great job miserable. An inward acknowledgment that the Lord has placed you under their authority will help your attitude. Focus on honoring that person; the Lord placed them in that position of authority. Honoring the position rather than the personality leads to a proper response to any type of leader you encounter in your career.

As an entry level technical trainee at Lanier, my supervisor had a quiet, yet demanding and superior personality. On one occasion, I earned lots of overtime on a government installation—pulling wire through an Army Hospital. He called me into his office and threw the check on the table as he said, "There's your check, you $@&! You aren't worth a penny of it!" I was pleased to receive this unexpected check and felt challenged to please my authority. However, it was demeaning to hear that comment since I had worked so hard. It helped that I deeply respected him for his technical and mechanical know-how. In my youth, I had been taught to respect authority, and I am so glad that I responded correctly to this first boss. I did not answer back but responded with a grateful and respectful attitude. It was much later when I understood the principle that the Lord directs us through our authorities.

When I transferred to the field for my work as a repairman, I inherited another boss that was really a source of irritation. Each day he reviewed my work and would often find one thing I had done wrong. He then proceeded to dress me down, never mentioning all the good things I had accomplished. A steady diet of that approach will drive you crazy, and I considered leaving to go back to college and change careers. Regardless of his approach, every day I continued to deliver excellent performance, productivity, and customer satisfaction. Soon I received a promotion, a perfect solution to my problem with this supervisor.

> *"If you think your boss is stupid, remember: You wouldn't have a job if he was any smarter."*
> —*John Gotti*

Continue to do the most effective, efficient job of which you are capable. If you allow your performance to suffer under a weak leader, you will not be promoted. A promotion earned can remove you from a difficult situation. Don't count on that, but it could happen when you are an outstanding performer.

In my first management assignment, my new boss was about as opposite from me as you could possibly imagine. He was single and had no regard for children. I was married with three children and deeply committed to my family. He was not religious and did not respect the Bible, nor did he respect anyone who did. It was evident that he thought I was not tough enough to be effective in a leadership role. Although he was bright and had many good ideas, he was not effective in implementation. I took advantage of his valuable ideas and used them to an advantage even when he did not.

In dealing with our employees, this boss did many things that were offensive. This even prompted me to make a list of things he did that I would never do or say to anyone. These negative observations plus his good, creative ideas were valuable to my career. Often learning what *not* to do can be just as important as learning what you should do. Once again, excellent productivity resulted in a promotion.

When the Harris Corporation acquired our company, I encountered a new management style, at least for me. It was called program management and was a highly developed skill which Harris had used primarily for engineering projects. It consisted of managing progress along a timeline with milestones and dates when projects should be completed. The use of PERT (program evaluation and review technology) charts was usually part of this process. It worked extremely well for development projects.

However, employees already in high-level management positions can find this system very aggravating. Mature managers prefer a "free rein" leadership style and work hard to maintain that privilege. It's sometimes called simultaneous loose-tight controls. The use of a technique called "management by objectives" is much more effective at this level. You give your leaders a great deal of freedom to make decisions and changes, trusting their good judgment. However, there are certain principles that are rigidly adhered to—boundaries that cannot be violated, objectives that must be achieved, especially those that are a definite requirement for success.

I made an effort to please my boss under the more difficult management style. But I must admit that I was pleased when he left to accept another job. Following him, I reported directly to the Chairman, Jack Hartley, who turned out to be one of the best bosses of my entire career. I knew that he trusted my judgment and respected me as a leader.

"Management by objective works—if you know the objectives.
Ninety percent of the time you don't."
— *Peter Drucker*

Prior to our being acquired by Harris Corporation, I had reported to Gene Milner for over 30 years. I was constantly pressured by him. It seemed he always had some comment, mostly sarcastic or demeaning. He was almost a foot taller than me and presented a commanding presence. Not only was he physically large, but he was loud and domineering. He loved to make brash comments that shocked those who heard. He was a master of exaggeration and loved to needle anyone he thought needed it. Needling was one of his primary methods of correction.

Needling our suppliers at the dealer meetings was one of Gene's greatest pleasures. Because our results were always outstanding, he could get away with it. Other dealers loved his barbed comments because Gene would say much of what they actually wanted to say. Of course, the suppliers disliked his tactics, and it cost us dearly in our relationships with them.

Out of necessity, I had to develop effective methods of approaching Gene in order to have any impact on the business. His instructions were, "If you need to know anything, just ask *me*. You simply stay out in the field making calls and training the managers." Gene had a unique twist on the Golden Rule. His often quoted version was, "He who has the gold makes the rule!"

When I presented any problem to Gene, he never discussed the alternatives with me. His quick response was, "Here's what you are to do." With such a forceful and dictatorial directive, I felt like his puppet rather than a co-worker. It became extremely important that I get my ideas on the table.

In time, I learned to present the solution before I described the problem. He frequently responded with positive consent. I further benefited from the conversation, as he would add suggestions that improved the decision. Gene had an uncanny sense of business, and I was often a benefactor of his wisdom. Using my improved approach gave me the freedom to put my ideas into action, make decisions, and benefit from his expertise. Regardless of a pleasing outcome, with this approach I seldom received credit or recognition.

When you make your boss' job easier, you increase your own worth and value in the workplace. Discover his or her goals, and do everything that you can to enable their achievement. Always seek to make up for your boss' weakness without being obvious. No matter what leadership style you may encounter, this is a rule for release.

Even though Gene almost never complimented me, he said a few things from time to time that let me know he had plans for my future. Once he said, "Wes, the other day I drove through Hiram, Georgia (my home town). I couldn't believe what I saw. On the water tank were the words—Hiram, Georgia, home of Wes Cantrell." At that time, Hiram didn't even have a water tank. It was heartening to know that this was his way of encouraging me.

Occasionally Gene seemed to notice my discouragement with his negative, criticizing leadership style. Once he commented, "I never waste my time picking spots out of rotten apples."

> *"Keep away from people who try to belittle your ambitions. Small people always do that, but the really great make you feel that you, too, can become great."*
> —Mark Twain

Any relationship with Gene was a combination of love and hate, much like the Green Bay Packers said about their relationship with Vince Lombardi: "We loved where he was taking us, but we hated the pressure and criticism that was his dominant leadership style." It also reminded me of what one player said of Bear Bryant: "His leadership style was a combination of abject fear and the hope of winning a national championship."

While conducting a Bible study on the life of Joseph, I asked myself the question "Is that why I am here?" His brothers sold Joseph into slavery, but he became second in command to Pharaoh. The Lord used Joseph to provide for His people. After many years, Joseph met the brothers who had sold him as a slave. In the closing scene of Genesis, as the truth of the situation unfolded, Joseph said, "You meant evil against me; but God meant it for good!" (Genesis 50:20). Through Joseph the entire nation of Israel was preserved. He was God's agent in a pagan land. His words rang loudly in my ears as I faced many trying issues. Joseph's summary statement was a great encouragement to me. It was often consoling to think that perhaps I could be that one man used of the Lord for His good in our company and the marketplace.

The pressure of a difficult boss made me more teachable as I listened and watched for spiritual solutions. One evening my wife and I went to hear a speaker who addressed the issue of dealing with a difficult boss. The apostle Peter dealt with this subject in a particularly direct way. He said, "Servants, be submissive to your masters with all fear, not only to the good and gentle, but also to the harsh. For this is commendable, if because of conscience toward God one endures grief, suffering wrongfully. For what credit is it if, when you are beaten for your faults, you take it patiently? But when you do good and suffer, if you take it patiently, this is commendable before God." (I Peter 2:18-20)

Peter reminds us again that we are to submit to all authorities the Lord has placed over us. The purpose of authority is to honor those who do well and to correct those who do wrong. When we do well under authority, it silences those who would accuse us unjustly. Freedom of choice is a glorious thing for the servant of the Lord, but we must never use this freedom as a license to respond incorrectly.

When our improper behavior is brought to our attention, we need to recall that it is the Lord speaking through that authority. Our correct and gracious response will be noticed, and quick correction will be noticed even more.

At times we suffer for doing good and are unjustly attacked for it. The Lord desires that we depend on Him. He will enable us to endure and respond graciously rather than react inappropriately. He is pleased when we respond with patience. Returning evil for evil only makes matters worse. No one gets promoted (released) when they display a defensive reaction. Peter instructs that we should respond correctly to our authorities whether they are kind and gentle or harsh and overbearing. When I learned the meaning of "harsh"—angry, cantankerous, and overbearing—I was sure that Peter knew Gene!

This penetrating spiritual truth of responding with respect even when mistreated greatly impacted me for present and future authorities. It brought new freedom to me. Peter's advice was exactly what I needed to hear. I had many opportunities to be obedient and respond correctly, not only to Gene but to other bosses as well.

We are often tempted to escape when we are in the molding and developing process. The Lord uses adversity to accelerate our spiritual maturity when we respond correctly. The potter's wheel is a Scriptural object lesson. Just imagine the clay leaping off the potter's wheel before the potter shapes the vessel. The Lord knows exactly what we need to fit into His plans. He will shape as He pleases—the willingness to conform is up to us. These lines from an old hymn written by Adelaide Pollard in 1907 paint a word picture of this yieldedness: "Have Thine own way Lord, have Thine own way. Thou art the potter, I am the clay. Mold me and make me after thy will, while I am waiting, yielded and still."

Having a difficult boss is certainly a trial. The emotional stress may become too much. You may seriously think about escape, but first, consider this caveat. If you work for a high-quality company, it is most likely that they will eventually replace a truly bad person who is in a leadership position. The problem will not remain secret, and top management will take the necessary action in time. Patience is the key, and avoiding undermining or discrediting your boss in words, actions, or attitudes is of great value. Escaping from the present discomfort may be a missed opportunity for spiritual growth, and you could escape into a far worse situation.

This is not to imply that there are never legitimate reasons to leave a job. One such scenario might be dishonesty in the ranks or dishonesty that is known and tolerated, perhaps even promoted by the leaders. It would be necessary to leave, but only after meeting with management and determining if correction is being considered. Your boss' superiors may ask you direct questions about your boss. In such cases you should answer honestly, making absolutely certain that you do not exaggerate or give an inaccurate report.

Many companies conduct what is called a 360-degree evaluation. They consult all those working below and above the individual, as well as his or her peers. They will ask questions in several different areas of competence and conduct. The general purpose is to create a plan for improvement for the subject individual. However, if the reports confirm a large amount of negative behavior, that person will be demoted or replaced. If you are consulted in such an evaluation, the proper attitude should always be one of contributing to a plan for growth and improvement. A vindictive or angry attitude will go against the contributor. In some cases, the offensive behavior is corrected. It would be wise to discuss the offensive behavior privately with the person being evaluated beforehand. Some people respond well to the chance to correct their behavior before a bad report is given.

An attractive job offer can be tempting when we are dissatisfied in our present job. The key word is *caution*! You cannot discover all you would like to know until you accept the offer. Then it's too late. However, there are certainly legitimate attractive offers that will come along that might be a better opportunity for you. Many people have significantly accelerated their careers by changing jobs. Just be aware of the "greener grass" syndrome. It might be artificial turf!

There is a major ethical point that is often encountered in this "change jobs or stay put" dilemma. Once you have agreed with the new employer regarding salary and benefits, your current employer may make a counteroffer to encourage you to stay. Once you give your word to your new employer, don't be tempted by any offer from your present company. If they were aware of your talents, why haven't they already given you a promotion or a raise? Give your word and stick to your commitment.

The **Key** of responding is certainly a major step in the process of releasing your CEO within. You will encounter many different bosses with a wide range of management styles. Reacting to your leaders negatively and seeking to escape will delay the release of your CEO within. When you respond correctly, many other pieces fall into place. If you don't respond correctly, you will not experience release of your true potential. Your responses and reactions are an important element in the development of your leadership abilities. This is true at home, in church, and in any organization or relationship. A great leader is first and foremost a great follower.

"A good follower in any situation is not a bump on a log. A good follower knows what needs to be done to make the leader most effective and does that without having to be told. A listener chooses behaviors that make the speaker most effective. In this way the listener is a follower actively supporting the lead of the speaker. When you're following, you're actually leading."
—*Unknown*

Chapter Three

The Key of Refining

Becoming a leader

As we were landing in St. Paul, Minnesota, I asked myself, "Why would anyone come here in the middle of winter?" Everything was covered with snow and ice! It was comforting to know that I had bought a new topcoat for the trip, one with a heavy lining.

Not only was I feeling the cold weather on the outside, I felt cold desperation inside. Having been recently promoted, I had no idea how to be a manager. The company offered no formal training, and my new boss had seemingly little interest in helping me. In short, I was facing failure as a manager. Hungry for advice and training, I held high hopes for this meeting at 3M headquarters. I was not disappointed.

The program, "Vision for Supervision," was taught by a couple of professors from the University of Minnesota and several top-level 3M managers. The three-day seminar had an immediate impact on my thinking and consequently my career. Anticipation grew as I returned to Baton Rouge and started putting into practice these most valuable lessons:

1. All development is self-development.
2. Never tolerate disloyalty.
3. Develop your own unique leadership style.

This was the beginning of a lifelong process, the development and continuing refinement of my management and leadership skills. Each of us must take personal responsibility for this KEY of releasing your CEO within: the KEY of refining. Many fail during the transition to management, and it almost happened to me. It is analogous to the catcher on a baseball team becoming the goalie on a hockey team. He's obviously a good athlete, but now he must learn to skate! New skills are required.

It was obvious that I was different from most of the successful company managers with whom I was acquainted. Several were loud, profane, extremely self-centered, heavy drinkers and womanizers, or so they said. The question dogged me: Did I have to become like them to be successful? In my gut, I did not feel that was necessary. What were the core attributes that dictated success in the business?

The training at 3M made me recall my first experience with learning how to sell. The transition from repair service to sales was tough. I had a good boss during that span of time, but training time with him was limited. If I was to learn how to sell, my development was mostly up to me. I read books, made calls, and conferred with my boss at every opportunity. The training conference reawakened the reality of my earlier experience. Self-development was the answer.

A major example of how self-development helped me in learning the sales business was the challenge of handling objections while learning to sell. In those early days, it seemed that I always said the wrong thing. In some cases I even argued with the prospect. "Winning the argument and losing the sale" became more than just an expression. My list of potential customers' objections grew, and I spent considerable time thinking of the best noncontroversial answers. Learning to convert an objection into a question was a rewarding experience. Practicing this new skill along with other techniques I had learned, it was not long until I began to get outstanding sales results.

One of the professors who conducted the 3M training used a phrase that stuck in my mind. He said that most young college graduates come to work on their first job with an attitude of "industrial Momism." In other words, "Here I am—take care of all my needs; make me successful!" With less than 2 percent of our time spent in training, self-development becomes a compelling focus. We must be willing and eager to learn. The professor emphasized over and over the individual responsibility for personal development in the job.

This principle was of tremendous personal value. Blaming my boss for his shortcomings in training was no longer an option and was at best a feeble excuse. I was convinced of my personal responsibility. Development was not something someone did to me, it was something I needed to do for myself. It was critical that I be willing to learn and that I be teachable. It was up to me to take action: to read, study, and take advantage of every training opportunity. I desired more exposure to those who had already developed the skills I needed to learn. I carefully sought out a few willing mentors, seasoned "old salts" who knew the ropes.

Throughout my career, I attended many management development programs and profited greatly from them. Some were sponsored by our company, and some I selected on my own. If you need an MBA to progress in your field, you can attend one of the executive development programs conducted by many colleges and universities. There are accelerated programs available, and many companies will give you time off and pay your tuition to attend such programs. In some organizations, those three letters—MBA—are a key for advancement and growth. If that is true in your work, get an MBA!

An important aspect of personal development is productive reading habits. You must learn new concepts and techniques. Reading books written by successful businessmen and noted management experts can be very helpful. Peter Drucker's *The Practice of Management* is outstanding and a must-read for everyone moving into management. Larry Burkett's *Business by the Book* is loaded with practical Biblical business principles.

When I speak to students, they frequently ask about my reading habits. My answer is, "If I could read only two things they would be the Bible and the *Wall Street Journal.*" Reading a chapter of Proverbs along with other segments of Scripture each day is a superb reading habit and one that has greatly benefited my life. Proverbs is full of great business advice as well as instruction on being a solid leader in the home. It's a wisdom-filled book. In my daily Bible reading, it is amazing how often I find the answer to a problem I'm currently facing. Reading from modern English translations such as the *New King James Version*, the *English Standard Version*, or the *New Living Translation* significantly improves comprehension and personal application. The website *www. blue letterbible.org* provides access to all these versions at no charge.

The *Wall Street Journal* is an educational business newspaper. When you read stories about other companies, you not only learn what to do, but often you learn what *not* to do. You will be up to date on current events, both in business and politics. The editorials are also excellent and quite educational.

Another valuable tool for self-development is the Internet. You can type any question into a search engine and get answers and resource materials. Basically, you have an entire library just a few clicks away that is segmented by subject.

Mentoring is a frequently used term in today's world. Mentoring is most effective when it is unsolicited and happens in the context of natural relationships. Your boss may not be a good mentor because he or she has a financial stake in your progress. The best mentor is one who takes a personal interest in your growth with no monetary motives of their own. Their motive is purely altruistic: to help you be successful with no strings attached. A good mentor can be a sounding board, advisor, teacher, and more. Typically, the mentor is older and more experienced than the mentee.

In my career, three older, more experienced men played a major role in my development. One was a fellow worker, one was an interested friend, and one was a higher level executive in our parent company. Their advice and friendships were priceless. Cultivate these types of relationships. You will grow to appreciate them more and more each year.

When I returned to Baton Rouge from the management development program in St. Paul, I knew I had to face the same challenging and unpleasant problem of disloyalty that I had temporarily left behind. The training instructor had made it perfectly clear that no one, no matter how skilled or productive they might be, should be allowed to remain on the job if they were not loyal to the company and to their leader. He explained that even though their personal production might be outstanding, they would impede the performance of others. Such a person would represent a "headwind" to the leader, undermining the vision and purpose that was being established. A disloyal person may even attempt to take over the agenda of an organization. If such a person is allowed to stay, it is perceived as weakness on the part of the leader.

When I began my new job in Baton Rouge, the top salesman in the entire company was under my supervision. His expressions and attitudes spoke loudly; he thought that he should have been given my position. He set out to get rid of me. By criticizing and undermining me, he was damaging the morale and productivity of the entire team.

After the confirming teaching I received at the conference, on the return trip I made the decision to fire him.

The Baton Rouge district literally took off once he was gone. The other employees had been watching and waiting for my response to this dilemma and rejoiced over my decision. My action made it clear. I was the leader and would take hard-hitting action to protect our mutual opportunity. Our performance was outstanding, and in just two years I was promoted to headquarters in a general management position. Without taking action on this difficult responsibility, I am fully convinced that I would have ultimately lost my job.

This one incident was not the end of my need to ferret out disloyalty. As I moved up through the ranks, there were many ambitious people who wanted my job and were willing to do almost anything to get it. Ambition is a good thing when it's based on performance and integrity. Nothing much has ever been accomplished without ambition. But when it is greedy, selfish, and grasping, and particularly when it involves destroying someone else's career, ambition is entirely wrong. The politics involved obstruct the performance of the entire operation and everyone suffers.

In one case, an ambitious manipulator won the favor of my boss and was making progress toward his goal of getting rid of me. His agenda and deceptive techniques were revealed when my boss conducted an exit interview with a highly respected employee. He said that this "manipulator" was his reason for leaving. My boss had thought highly of the "manipulator," but was now convinced of his vicious intent and fired him. This was a great relief—a straightforward way of convincing the boss of the malicious intent of this individual.

Our business employed many fine Christians who were dependable, productive workers. However, one particular Christian executive taught me yet another lesson about disloyalty and destructive ambition. He became more arrogant, superior, and prideful as the company grew and he received promotions. I made a serious mistake: I overly depended on his Christian character to convict him and lead him to correct his disloyal behavior.

Such behavior must be confronted head-on, even with Christians. Quoting Scripture may not be effective, especially if your adversary is blinded by selfish ambition. In fact, we must manage Christians essentially the same way as everyone else. Establishing guidelines or requirements regarding behavior, loyalty, communication, and other factors is a *must*. Confrontation is mandatory when the expectations are not met. If the employee does not make corrections, he or she must be terminated. In hindsight, I must now acknowledge this painful lesson and its great cost to our organization.

Those who are destructively ambitious are usually deceptively clever and may be difficult to readily recognize. There were a few signals I observed with this individual, but I chose not to address. There was a lack of enthusiasm for projects that didn't originate with this ambitious leader. There was unusual questioning of my decisions and in some cases a visit with a "bad report from his people"—an attempt to use the threat of numbers to bring pressure. Employees in a disloyal executive's line of authority are fearful and seldom will express their opinion under his authority. That was certainly true in this case. No longer having that fear when they leave, employees will often provide truthful, valuable information in their exit interviews.

Typically, a disloyal person will not participate in your staff meetings except as a "command performance" which you schedule. They show little support for your new ideas and leadership. They seem to support only ideas that they originate. They are not supportive of your staff members, particularly those who might question their underhanded methods or expose them. Deceptively clever, ambitious people can produce results, and leaders tend to overlook the revealing signals because of their performance. As soon as you observe any or all of these signals, it's time to take action.

The third major lesson I took home from the program in St. Paul involved developing your own unique leadership style. Previously, I had thought that management meant forcing people to do what you want them to do. My experience with threatening, demanding, and intimidating management was uncomfortable, but it was all I had known. Readily, I was sold on the idea of an effective leader convincing followers to *want* to do what must be accomplished with a shared vision of the future. I welcomed the thought of pleasant and harmonious teamwork with a mutual objective. In thoughtfully considering this new definition of leadership, I recognized the tremendous possibilities. This was the way to unleash enthusiasm and energy—the key to great productivity. Thus began my lifelong development process of refining my leadership ability. Developing leadership ability is a KEY for release, and it is not optional.

"What makes leadership is the ability to get people to do what they don't want to do and like it."
—*Harry Truman*

Viewing leadership as a special gift rather than a developing skill is misleading. As I reviewed my career, I realized that I had been developing leadership abilities all along, as I am sure that you have been doing. I thought of times in my life when I had convinced others to support my position, even though it was not intuitively obvious and seemed more difficult. Perhaps you need to correct your view of yourself as well. Even though earlier I had ruled out myself as a leader, my introspection was reassuring.

Experience in service and sales had been greatly beneficial to me. The persuasiveness I developed as a sales rep was now a part of my style. Along the same lines, I faced the facts about appearance. People make quick judgments based on appearance; therefore, our outward appearance is important. Being transparent and exposing your heart to others becomes the more valuable aspect. Make it easy for those who are following your leadership to read your heart. Leadership is the foundation of all great accomplishments. Without leadership, nothing much happens.

"The key to successful leadership today is influence, not authority."
—*Ken Blanchard*

The cornerstone of leadership is integrity. You must keep all promises, stick to the truth even when it hurts, and build a reputation of absolute dependability. Direct and frequent communication is a must. This builds trust, and your employees must trust you. Integrity builds trust.

In most organizations, there is an understood authority that comes with position. However, the truly great leader establishes moral authority based on integrity. Moral authority goes beyond position and is established when your people see that you personally keep the standards you set for others. It has been called alignment between "creed and deed," what you say compared to what you do. Remember, "The integrity of the upright guides them, but the crookedness of the treacherous destroys them." (Proverbs 11:3)

A study conducted by Watson Wyatt Worldwide revealed that shareholder returns were 42 percent higher in companies where employees trusted top executives. Sadly, only one-half of the employees surveyed trusted their senior managers.

> *"If you have integrity, nothing else matters. If you don't have integrity, nothing else matters!"*
> —*Alan Simpson, former US senator*

In my development as a manager, I realized that I had combined the functions of management and leadership. I needed to resolve the question, "What is the difference between management and leadership?"

A manager who develops good leadership skills becomes a more effective manager, but I had to master a deeper understanding of these two functions in order to continue developing leadership skills. I discovered several important aspects of each function.

Management involves more of a short-term focus. A manager is to check productivity on an incremental basis; solve the immediate problem today. Management is the day-to-day process of moving the organization along the charted path to achieve the desired results. It includes the skill of delegation, selecting people of competence and character to trust with major operations. On the other hand, leadership is a long-term function. A leader establishes strategy and purpose, understands the core processes of the business, and anticipates and prepares for change. The primary difference between a manager and a leader is foresight—being able to visualize changes that are coming in the future and establish strategy for the organization that takes advantage of change. Individuals must evaluate themselves and make the critical choice. Moving up (releasing your CEO within) requires leadership skills because leaders must deal effectively with strategy and change.

As a manager, I checked to make sure employees came to work on time, I looked at daily productivity measures that were critical to our success, and I made regular customer contacts. Hicks Lanier always said, "There is no fertilizer like the boss's footprints," and I understood that message. Two things were clear: I had to understand the customers' use of our products, and my associates would only respect what I inspected.

In my management position, there were long-term issues that needed to be brought to the attention of my associates. There were issues like establishing long-term goals that were based on increasing revenue, customer satisfaction, and annual incentive programs. There was our ranking as compared to other district offices in our region. Each rep needed encouragement to establish personal goals that would drive their performance on a longer-term basis, not just for the moment. There were family needs that had to enter into individual planning. Many had ambitions for promotion. Selecting and preparing those high potential individuals who might fit into future plans is great for assuring long-term performance. In addition, it develops your skill of delegation, a major requirement for effective leadership.

When I learned my boss's future plans, I brought the employees into the picture. I was aware of the future plan that one day our company would be a major force in the industry. All employees would benefit from the growth resulting from their excellent long-term performance. Without realizing that sharing the vision was a fundamental basis of leadership, I began to do the natural, common-sense thing. Sharing the vision demonstrated great promise for every employee throughout the entire organization. Enthusiasm and productivity soared. When coupled with the proper incentives and recognition, there were unparalleled outcomes.

"Where there is no vision, the people perish."
—*King Solomon*

Management experience offers a marvelous opportunity for leadership development. A good leader is always a better manager. A manager is most effective when leadership qualities are developed "on the job." This speeds the release of your CEO within. Perhaps there will be an opportunity to move into a higher level of leadership that involves pure strategy and change.

When I became a national sales manager later in my career, much of my work was with dealers. This gave me a welcomed opportunity to learn another aspect of leadership. Dealers were independent owners, and we had little, if any, authority over them. We could cancel their contract for non-payment, but we had no power over them. They were demanding and quick to criticize. They were generally slow adopters waiting for others to bruise their shins before getting involved in new programs we proposed.

Working with dealers gave me no choice; I had to learn to lead without authority. What a great lesson because it works even when you have absolute authority. I learned to lead from a platform of influence, using the power of persuasion. I learned to think of others as volunteers rather than "direct reports." Throwing your weight around, using threats, and intimidation are totally ineffective methods for moving others to a sustainable course of action. It is far better to convince them to desire with their whole heart what needs to be accomplished. Sometimes that can be a tough task.

In sports and racing, the purpose is winning and that is easy to explain. In business, your purpose must be clearly defined, and you must be able to communicate it. Develop leadership speeches and anecdotes that stimulate a desire for involvement in that purpose.

Leadership stories make an effective case and are often actual events that took place within the organization.

Deliver dramatic leadership speeches in order to persuade, prepare for change, unify, and align your followers. Develop such stories and learn to communicate effectively. There are numerous historical examples of great leadership stories. Many resulted in producing a dramatic change of direction on the part of large groups of people.

For example, on March 23, 1775, in Virginia, the largest colony in America, a meeting of the colony's delegates was held in St. John's Church in Richmond. Patrick Henry presented resolutions putting the colony of Virginia "into a posture of defense . . . embodying, arming, and disciplining such a number of men as may be sufficient for that purpose." Before the vote was taken on his resolutions, Henry delivered a speech imploring the delegates to vote in favor. Following his speech, the vote was taken. His resolutions passed by a narrow margin, and thus Virginia joined in the American Revolution. He spoke without any notes in a voice that became louder and louder, climaxing with the now famous ending and the part that every American knows!

"It is in vain, sir, to extenuate the matter. Gentlemen may cry, 'Peace! Peace!' But there is no peace. The war is actually begun! The next gale that sweeps from the north will bring to our ears the clash of resounding arms! Our brethren are already in the field! Why stand we here idle? What is it that gentlemen wish? What would they have? Is life so dear, or peace so sweet, as to be purchased at the price of chains and slavery? Forbid it, Almighty God! I know not what course others may take; but as for me, give me liberty, or give me death!" —Patrick Henry

Historians generally agree that the game-changer of World War II was Sir Winston Churchill. He demonstrated an iron will, fierce determination, and eloquent speech to motivate and encourage the people of England. The following is taken from one of his radio addresses after the *Luftwaffe* attacked London, causing massive destruction:

"Do not speak of darker days . . . Let us speak rather of sterner days. These are not dark days; these are great days—the greatest days our country has ever lived; and we shall all thank God that we have been allowed, each one of us according to our stations, to play a part in making these days memorable." —Winston Churchill

One might also think of Martin Luther King Jr.'s "I Have a Dream" speech as another great leadership speech. There are many examples in history, business, and Christianity. The Apostle Paul's speech at Mars Hill is another example of addressing a difficult audience with radical new thoughts. When addressing a somewhat hostile audience, it helps to find common ground to put them at ease.

Great leaders prepare carefully and deliver convincing leadership speeches. Even those who are not great orators can still be effective when they carefully craft their content and exhibit personal commitment with enthusiasm. Preparation is a requirement. When giving such a speech, frequently mention the organization's purpose. This reiteration keeps the purpose foremost in the minds of listeners. Quotes and stories that graphically illustrate key points are especially effective. Throughout my career I used *The Little Brown Book of Anecdotes*. I highly recommend it. Also, the Internet is a great source of quotes and other illustrative stories.

It has been said that the three most important aspects of real estate investments are location, location, and location. In the same fashion, the three most important aspects of leadership are communication, communication, and communication. There are many ways to communicate—newsletters, video, email, impromptu speeches, and one-on-one meetings. Use every available avenue to maximize effectiveness.

As CEO, I recorded a video each quarter which was to be viewed by all employees. Today the Internet would be used for a live web-cast. The purpose of the video was to answer three questions shared by all fellow workers: As a company, where are we headed? What is our present condition? What are the challenges and changes we are facing?

Some believe there would be no need for leadership if it were not for change. Although this is not entirely accurate, change demands leadership, or else the organization will fail to make necessary changes in a timely manner. The cognitive ability on the part of the leader to anticipate change and prepare an organization for it is a prerequisite for effective leadership. No matter what's ahead, if it is recognized and adjustments are made in advance, any change can be accommodated.

Sooner or later, there are three kinds of change that come to most organizations: reorganization, evolving technology, and mergers and/

or acquisitions. In all three of these situations, preparation of the work force is vital. Communicating the individual and organizational benefit is of utmost importance.

In most cases, training will be necessary to accommodate change. This is particularly true of technology. Information systems must be updated to take advantage of new systems that reduce cost. Everyone must be trained on the new system. In many cases there is a corresponding head-count reduction, which is always difficult to handle. If the technology change occurs in your company's products, the support force must be trained as well as the sales and marketing organization. A convincing speech without the backup of training and support will fail every time. Conversely, all the training and support could easily fail if the work force is not receptive to the change. Bringing every employee to receptiveness is the specific job of the leader.

A major part of every leader's responsibility is setting priorities. The old cliché to "keep the main thing the main thing" is still accurate and important. The secret of outstanding performance in any organization is proper focus. Organizations often stray from their strengths and expand into areas where they have no leverage. It is the leader's job to establish and maintain a strategic framework for the organization.

The million-dollar idea for leadership is incredibly simple: Each day, determine the single most important thing that needs to be completed that day. Don't quit until it is done. Even if other things are left undone, the most important task will be completed and the organization will thrive.

In Jim Collin's book *Good to Great,* he describes the surprising attributes of the best leaders, those who have consistently produced outstanding performance. "We were surprised, shocked really, to discover the type of leadership required for turning a good company into a great one. Compared to high-profile leaders with big personalities who make headlines and become celebrities, the good-to-great leaders seem to have come from Mars. Self-effacing, quiet, reserved, even shy, these leaders are a paradoxical blend of personal humility and professional will. They are more like Lincoln and Socrates than Patton or Caesar."

This is not a new discovery but was revealed by Jesus over 2,000 years ago. Jesus dealt with competitiveness, superiority, and inflated egos as He personally developed His staff (disciples). He even had to deal with an ambitious mother! The mother of James and John came to Jesus and inquired if her sons could have the two top slots as Jesus came into His kingdom. It was obvious that she did not realize what she was asking, but Jesus gave an instructive answer: "It is not Mine to give but it shall be given to them for whom it is prepared of my Father." The other staff members were incensed at this request and argued amongst themselves as to who would be the greatest. Jesus called them aside for a leadership training session. He delivered a leadership speech that was extremely important for them—and for us.

He told them that when those in the secular world are promoted, they often become controlling, order-shouting tyrants wanting everyone to know: "I'm in charge here!" But believers are not to be that way. We are to lead by serving, serving our staff, customers, associates, and shareholders. "He who wants to be greatest of all should be servant of all!" Jesus then said that He came not to be served, but to serve and to offer His life as a ransom for many (Matthew 20:20-28). Jesus led by loving and serving: "Greater love has no one than this, than to lay down one's life for his friends." (John 15:13) The hallmark of the true servant leader: He is more concerned for the success of his leader and his followers rather than his own success.

> *"When you are in a position of authority and your followers do not obey, the blame does not lay with them but with you! It is a spiritual problem—get right with God!"*
> —Oswald Chambers

Many books are being written about servant-leadership. It is not a new discovery; it was prescribed and demonstrated by Jesus over 2,000 years ago. There's a lot said about this subject in the Scriptures. The Bible is the major source for refining your leadership skills. All education dims in comparison to God's Word. Partake of it each day and speed the release of your CEO within!

Chapter Four

Currency or Character

God's purpose for wealth

During my childhood years, my parents arose by 5:30 a.m. and entered the kitchen to prepare breakfast. The enticing aroma of bacon wafted to my room, but I wouldn't give up the comfort of my bed. Also, in those early morning hours, I was privy to conversations that my parents never knew I heard.

Our old country home had no insulation. The cold or hot outside air seeped through the thin walls. I could easily hear every word my parents exchanged in those early morning conversations. A major subject was the need for money. There were always bills to pay or house repairs that were needed, and many such subjects were discussed. Through this eavesdropping education, I began to realize that my desire to have anything other than the bare necessities would not be possible unless I, myself, earned income. I made a decision; I would not be poor. Although it was unknown to me at the time, that was a profound commitment that would have a detrimental impact on my life.

Influenced by that commitment, I was working to make money by the time I entered seventh grade. I did bicycle repairs for neighborhood boys. I even built a bicycle from used parts and sold it at a small profit. Before long, I had a paper route in the afternoon, the *Atlanta Journal*, and later added the morning route, the *Atlanta Constitution*. It was the only time in my business career I had a monopoly. I loved it!

On Saturdays, I greased and washed cars at the local filling station. Chicken farming was an important community business, and I had many jobs related to that industry. My mother hated my smelly clothes, but I appeased her by saying that I was the champion chicken catcher of Paulding County. These jobs enabled me to buy most of my own clothes and pay for the extra things I wanted. I always had money and even made short-term loans to some of the other boys in school.

These were healthy experiences with lots of hard work, and in most cases I was interfacing directly with customers. Although unaware, I was developing a good work ethic. Unfortunately, I also developed an unbalanced desire for money. Everyone needs money, but when it occupies the top priority in your life, there's trouble ahead.

Often we read accounts of contemporary corporations where a few leaders have demonstrated the unbridled desire for money. These disasters could have been avoided if these leaders had adopted a proper view of the Source of all things. With a selfish view, there is always the potential of bondage to the love of money.

The profit motive is a necessity, and the free-market system wouldn't survive without it. However, when there is a character deficit, the profit motive can morph into an ugly thing—greed. Incentives work quite well in a free-market environment, but they can be horribly distorted by the love of money.

While in high school, I thought about the idea of working for commissions frequently. But for me, only a guaranteed salary was acceptable. That attitude was based on my childhood experiences. The security of guaranteed income was important to me.

When I was working as a customer service rep, I noticed that the sales reps earned more money and seemed to work at a more leisurely pace. I was attracted to the idea of more money and the unlimited potential for income based on production. My childhood idea regarding a guaranteed income was beginning to change.

When the company offered relocation to Gulfport, Mississippi, as a combination sales/service rep, I eagerly accepted the offer. Since I had no sales experience or training, I struggled to learn how to sell. With lots of determination and the support of a loving wife, I began to do quite well.

After only two enjoyable years on the Gulf Coast, the company transferred me to Augusta, Georgia. Some time later my production declined and I was definitely in a slump. My enthusiasm fell along with my production, and my work ethic suffered. There was no leadership present in Augusta; I was the leadership! I was stranded with no counselor, advisor, or helper.

One Sunday afternoon, two leaders from our church made a surprise visit. They knew nothing of my dilemma, but in the course of our conversation they suggested that we should be tithing. This was counter to all my thinking. How could I give more when I had only made $262 the previous month?

We had often heard our pastor say, "There is a direct connection between a man's wallet and his heart." Considering what he taught and what these men had carefully presented, we made a decision to give 10 percent of our gross income to the Lord's work. The decision to tithe, although we were already under tremendous financial stress, was one of the foundational building blocks for the rest of my life and career. This verse holds great promise for the giver with a good attitude about giving. "Remember this—a farmer who plants only a few seeds will get a small crop. But the one who plants generously will get a generous crop. You must each decide in your heart how much to give. And don't give reluctantly or in response to pressure. For God loves a person who gives cheerfully." (II Corinthians 9:6-7 NLT)

The decision to give regardless of our circumstances was an enlightening step toward many changes in my attitude about money. Were my efforts to be dominated by the desire for money or would I be more concerned with my character? Would my life be focused on wealth—or wisdom? The decision to tithe established the fact that the unsurpassed antidote for greed is giving. From this newly established pattern, I learned about the Lord's promise of blessing to those who give. His blessing is abundant with a special measure of contentment, and it may or may not include material wealth (I Timothy 6:6).

"You're never more like Jesus than when you're giving."
—Johnny Hunt

Giving became more of an issue as my income began to grow. Moving into higher level jobs provided more money, and we were socializing frequently with wealthy people. In other words, there was more temptation to return to old habits. There were lavish trips with fine clothes and jewelry on display for comparison. There was that ever-present temptation to simply go for the money, power, and prestige! I frequently dealt with the distraction of money-related issues.

Larry Burkett, the founder of Christian Financial Concepts, became a dear friend. He encouraged me to understand the many things the Scripture tells us about money. In fact there are more than 584 verses in the Bible that deal with money. That alone shows us how important it is to establish our thoughts regarding money from the Lord's perspective. Most of these verses are warnings about the misuses of money.

"One-fifth of all Jesus had to say was about money!"
—Billy Graham

I Timothy 6:5-12 greatly impacted my thinking about money. In these verses, we find the following powerful lessons.

- We should not be misled by making lots of money and confuse this with Godliness. (v. 5)
- We should separate ourselves from those who believe this false sign of God's blessing—that monetary prosperity is God's blessing. (v. 5)
- We cannot take our wealth with us. (v. 7) Others will enjoy what we worked so hard to accumulate. (Proverbs 5:10)

"There is no reason to be the richest man in the cemetery. You can't do any business from there."
–Colonel Sanders

- We should be content with the basic necessities of life. God has promised to provide for our basic needs. Contentment is the best evidence of Godliness. (v. 6, 8)
- The desire to be rich is a trap that leads to destruction. (v. 9)

- The love of money is exceptionally powerful and is a root motive in all evil. The motive involves a craving that leads away from devotion and brings mental anguish. (v. 10)
- Those who place their happiness in wealth are subject to Satan's snares. Qualities evoked by materialism lead to many other problems. When Satan sees which way lusts are leading, he baits his hook accordingly. Greed pulls one away from a devoted walk with the Lord. (v. 10)
- People may have money and yet not love it. Some of God's great men of the Bible were wealthy. A few of these are Abraham, Isaac, Job, David, Zacchaeus (the wealthy tax collector who gave half of his wealth to the poor after he met Jesus), and Joseph of Arimathea.

In my struggle to win completely over my desire to make lots of money, I had to examine the question, "What is driving me in my work?" Was my motive to serve others and be prosperous so that I might give to God's work? Was I working to make more and more money at the expense of my family and my relationship with the Lord? Or was I just being diligent? These are thoughts that should be a caution for anyone. Introspection with honest answers became acutely necessary. The choice was clear and the caution great. I knew that I might have wealth, but I didn't want wealth to have me. Matthew 6:24 explains, "No one can serve two masters, for either he will hate the one and love the other, or he will be devoted to the one and despise the other. You cannot serve God and money." NLT

> *"He does not possess wealth that allows it to possess him."*
> —*Benjamin Franklin*

Once each year I met with my boss to discuss salary and bonus plans. Most of my peers advised me to negotiate strongly. I did not heed that advice because I knew I was actually working for the Lord, and He is the One who paid me (Colossians 3:24). My approach became one of prayer—not for the Lord to give me specific amounts, but that those making the decision would be prompted by the Lord to pay me as He directed. Trusting Him (not man or my own negotiations) left me with even more contentment and many thrilling and surprising answers to that prayer. Good and even bitter medicines go down smoothly when you know the Source is the Lord!

When Harris Corporation became our parent company, I was given the largest raise in my career. Harris recognized that I was underpaid based on their competitive wage data. They corrected that immediately. This was an unexpected and welcomed blessing of the Lord. It was also reassuring to know the new owners approved of my performance and potential.

Wealth can have an incredible impact on a marriage relationship. In working with many other couples, my wife and I easily observed that much conflict and many divorces resulted from arguments about finances. Bernadine and I never had that problem. From the beginning of our marriage, we had one joint bank account. We considered that everything we had was ours, not "yours" and "mine." As we learned Biblical financial principles, we were always in agreement.

While walking down the hall one day, my boss and I were discussing our wives. He had married the daughter of one of the founders, and she had been raised with wealth. As I commented on my wife and her work around the house, he looked at me, thoughtfully analyzing what I had said. Then he explained, "Your wife didn't come into the marriage with wealth as mine did." I replied, "Oh yes, she did; she had lots of stock!" With a disbelieving scowl, he asked, "What kind of stock?" My reply: "About 22 head!" Gene had a great sense of humor, and we had a good laugh together.

My wife's parents were graciously generous even though they were not wealthy. Often her dad mentioned selling one of Bernadine's cows in order to meet one of our needs, especially as our children were born. Being puzzled over the number of cows Bernadine owned, I asked my father-in-law, "Just how many cows does she own?" He gave me a fuzzy answer, which I interpreted to mean that whenever we had a need, she owned another cow!

When each of our children was born, Bernadine's parents always gave a cash gift and encouraged us to establish a savings account for that child. From their example, we saw the wisdom of saving for the children. II Corinthians 12:14 states, "The children ought not to lay up for the parents, but the parents for the children."

We continued the process that Bernadine's parents began. We put money into the children's savings accounts until they entered college. Then we gave them total access to their account. We had taught them financial principles, and this was their time to become overseers of their own financial activity. Each one purchased a car and paid college expenses with the savings started by Bernadine's parents. We made it through our children's college years with no financial stress. In addition, the children had no debt when they graduated. Today all four of our children are financially sound and are good money managers. What a blessing!

Establishing college funds to help your children is one thing. Paying taxes is another! When taxes are due, greed has another chance to rear its ugly head. Perhaps greed can be characterized as any motive to get without giving or investing—*keeping* what you have or *taking* from others.

When it comes to taxes, greed falls in the category of *keeping*. I resented paying more taxes as my income increased, so I looked for the so-called tax shelter. The most advantageous tax shelters had the highest risk. Even though I was not a tax lawyer, I could see that many of these tax avoidance schemes would not survive IRS scrutiny. Although I felt it was not the wisest thing to do, I took the risk. I went against my wife's advice and paid dearly for the decision to "keep."

Working for commissions, bonuses, or owning a business offers temptation and opportunity for cheating. Greed is characterized by the desire to take or keep what is not rightfully yours. Most people do not succumb to *taking* because they remember that old saying "crime doesn't pay." That is definitely true because crime always bears unpleasant consequences in the long term. With that in mind, why are so many involved in crime? Crime does pay handsomely in the near term. Criminals likely do not consider consequences as strongly as they consider the power, prestige, and prosperity of "taking" what does not belong to them. The Mafia is the most profitable organization in the world! As a far-fetched example, I shudder to think what would happen if they went public and sold stock in their business. No doubt all the stock would be sold out before the close of business the first day.

The desire to get rich quickly by breaking the rules is a tempting incentive and it is rationalized by thinking, "I'm too smart to get caught!" Proverbs makes it clear that "get rich quick" schemes are to be avoided (28:20, 22). We have all read of several public companies whose leaders broke the rules in order to get rich quickly. Overstating earnings and backdating stock options are nothing more than changing the truth into a lie. Proverbs 21:6 (NIV) says it well: "A fortune made by a lying tongue is a fleeting vapor and a deadly snare."

Taking a company public is an exhilarating experience. Shortly after our stock started trading, we were in the World Trade Center with the chairman of an investment banking firm. We were on the 60th floor and I was looking out on the harbor and the Statue of Liberty. It seemed that I could see the entire world from that vantage point and I felt an overwhelming sense of importance. Wall Street can get in your blood—there is great temptation in the trade center of the world. The promise of fortunes and the "thrill of the deal" are major enticements. Wealth and power are intoxicating. The temptation came into my thoughts subtly and quickly. My choice was not to linger there but to remember, "The eyes of man are never satisfied." (Proverbs 27:20) The right choice is to focus on the Lord who owns it all! Jesus said, "What profit is it to a man if he gains the whole world, and loses his own soul? Or what will a man give in exchange for his soul? (Matthew 16:26)

Ron Blue, a financial counselor and friend, uses a phrase that speaks volumes: "Cap your lifestyle." As we listened to one of his presentations, Bernadine and I were pleased that we had made that decision several years before. We knew that Ron was on target with that expression. We had observed many of our acquaintances in high places who were awfully busy keeping up with their new toys. Two or three houses, elaborate trips, expensive automobiles, and other personal indulgences were the topics of most of their conversations. Many of our casual friends' social lifestyles became a showcase for their wealth—prestige, parties, and possessions.

We proceeded with caution as we sought the Lord's direction about possessions and how we were to use the money that He provided. Aware that appearance is important for the CEO of a publicly held company,

I also knew that possessions could be taken to the extreme in an effort to impress others.

---

*"Theirs is an endless road, a hopeless maze, who seek for goods
before they seek for God"*
—*Bernard of Clairvaux*

Our decision was to give away the surplus. We aspired to gradually increase our giving to the Lord's work, both through our local church and worldwide evangelistic and missionary activities. With concern for our extended family of four children and their large families, we also made a decision about gifts to our children. We have placed more value in contributing to their current needs than having them wait for the reading of the will.

As has so often been the case in our lives, the Lord gave us guidelines for giving through Mike Gilchrist, an evangelist and dear friend.

- Always give to God—not to man or causes.
- Always give from God's resources—not your own.
- Always give by revelation—not reason.

These continue to be our guidelines for giving. We recognize that we are "only conveyors of His resources." Proverbs 21:26 explains, "[The wicked] are always greedy for more, while the Godly love to give!"

It is wise to include retirement plans in your financial considerations. I have never met anyone who wished to retire without resources. Most corporations and individuals invest effort, time, and thought into enabling employees to retire more comfortably. Even with individual planning, saving, and working toward appropriate financial goals, many do not find retirement comfortable. Many people think of retirement as a time to relax and enjoy life. They have decided that their years of service and work will be complete upon retirement. They will have new objectives, such as golf and a single-digit handicap, an impressive boat, a luxurious second home, and fun in the sun! Their retirement life will be devoted to travel and leisure. Their dedication to the accumulation of wealth is to ensure a dream life of ease.

Retirees will experience many disappointments if a life of leisure is their goal. Many are miserable. Even with achieving their dream, they discover that they don't enjoy being with their spouse or other acquaintances much of the time. To find contentment, some seek a significant or even insignificant job in order to get away.

A wife whose husband had recently retired expressed one perspective. She said, "I now have half as much money and twice as much husband!" Another said, "I love my husband all the time, just not for lunch!" My wife says, "I love having him with me all the time," and I believe she means it!

Many retirees have an identity crisis. High-level executives might suffer a dreadful blow to their ego because of the loss of status. The former CEO is just another person at the party and no longer identified by position. For anyone whose significance and identity are found only in their vocation, change is unsettling, dissatisfying, and there is an unrelenting void that dogs their everyday life. They focus on their yesterdays and are handicapped by their failures, or they spend their time bragging about their past successes.

My vocation was a great joy to me because I knew I was doing what God purposed for me to do. Even though I'm retired, He still has a purpose for me—He is not finished with me! My self-acceptance is not dependent on my rank at work, but on knowing who I am in Christ.

Folks often ask me what I miss most about my job. I jokingly answer, "Well, that check every two weeks would be the first thing. The corporate jet would be the second." These days, travel is such a hassle and flying commercial sometimes seems to be a form of torture. The question does occur to me sometimes, "What are all these people doing on my airplane?"

But seriously, I genuinely miss many of the people I worked with. There were some great folks at Lanier. Secondly, I miss having an assistant. I've had to learn to use the computer, particularly word processing. Another thing that is absent, the pressure of quarterly earnings releases. I don't miss that at all!

As Bernadine and I started to plan for retirement, we studied the Scriptures to see what the Lord had to say about the subject. We found only one mention. In Numbers 8:25, the priests retired from conducting their regular service at 50 years of age, but they continued to serve in other ways. The central thought here is that you never stop serving even though you've retired. We are continuing with our physical work in maintaining our home. We are serving, teaching, mentoring, and writing. We are always "on call" if the Lord opens a door of service and ministry.

Since I had established my identity long before retirement, I'm not suffering from an identity crisis now. My contentment is based on knowing who I am in Christ, not in being a CEO. We are having some of the richest experiences of our entire life. Our slogan is, "We want to die with our running boots on!"

A non-profit we are involved with held a board meeting at our house. One of our fellow directors had invested in Atlanta real estate and built a major shopping center and hotel in the center of an affluent area. He is an extremely wealthy man. Through fellowship with the board members and casual conversation, he learned about our stable marriage and our large, loving family. He had experienced many disappointments in his personal life and is married to his third wife.

By the end of the meeting, he looked at me and said, "Wes, you're the richest man I know!" Considering his financial status, this statement made a lasting impression on me. It also underscored what's really important in this life and what we should consider as true riches.

Many such experiences have prompted me to rethink my philosophy regarding wealth and its purpose. My direction in life changed from the pursuit of wealth to the pursuit of wisdom—from currency to character.

Consider these helpful hints as you examine your perspective of wealth. Hopefully, they may prevent some of the "hard knocks" of learning that were in my path. I would love to have begun my career with this higher-road thinking.

1. Investigate the Scriptures regarding money—it contains over 500 verses on the subject.

2. Distinguish between an honest profit motive and greed.

3. Become a giver, not a taker. The antidote for greed is giving and gratitude.

4. Protect against the "love of money"—the desire to be rich is a trap.

5. Money is not necessarily a sign of Godliness—the true blessing of the Lord is contentment.

6. Trust the Lord for your income. It is ultimately Him who supplies your every need. (Colossians 3:24)

7. Pay your taxes cheerfully!

8. Cap your lifestyle and give away the surplus.

9. Focus on true riches.

Your concept of wealth is critical to the release of your CEO within. Money and wealth will always be involved in your work. Jesus asked a probing question: "If you have not been trustworthy in handling worldly wealth, who will trust you with true riches?" (Luke 16:11 NIV) Remember, we always conform our lives to that which we love. The love of money generates a greedy, grasping, selfish person. "The trustworthy will get a rich reward. But the person who wants to get rich quick will only get into trouble." (Proverbs 28:20 NIT) Recognizing that wealth is God's resource yields contentment and joy.

> *"He that loseth wealth loseth much, he that loseth friends, loses more; but he that loseth his spirit loseth all!"*
> *—Spanish proverb*

Chapter Five

The Key of Reproducing

Building with the best

Our company had just gone public on the NYSE and we were flying high—literally. Our new company jet was taking us to Westchester, New York, late Sunday night for an early Monday meeting. The weather was awful and we couldn't see anything outside the airplane. We bounced up and down, and the plane lurched from side to side. It was a terrifying situation as we faced the reality that our lives depended on the skill of the pilots.

Jack, one of the pilots, looked back and said, "Hey Mr. Milner, we've got some $65,000 weather up here!" Then I remembered. Several months earlier, my boss demonstrated new confidence in my judgment when he gave me the assignment of hiring the pilots. I soon learned that the most important requirement for a pilot is time at the controls, actually flying the aircraft. The more hours of flying experience, the more valuable we considered the pilot. A pilot's value was enhanced if he had flown the same type of aircraft that our company would be using. There is no better indicator of future performance than previous performance.

My focus in the interviewing process was the pilot's proven competence, but I also asked probing questions to learn about his character. What about habits after work hours? What about home life? What problems might occupy his or her mind and hinder the need to focus on safety? Is there any evidence of a drinking problem?

Often when interviewing, the pilots asked about compensation. Jack had made the comment, "The worst thing that can happen is to have a $35,000-a-year pilot at the controls flying into $65,000-a-year weather!" Flying safely through the storm and securely landing in Westchester gave me the satisfied feeling of knowing we had made the best decision. Hiring these higher-paid, highly skilled pilots was the right choice.

This experience confirmed again that competence and character are the most important aspects of bringing in new talent or promoting from within. True success will depend on both these factors, and adequate compensation attracts qualified applicants.

> *"If you pick the right people and give them the opportunity to spread their wings—and put compensation as a carrier behind it—you almost don't have to manage them."*
> —Jack Welch

Reproducing the "best of breed"—hiring and promoting the best people in order to build a great organization—is critically important. It is wise to take the view that every hire holds the potential of life or death for the organization. In his book *Good to Great,* Jim Collins correctly states, "People are not your most valuable asset! Only the *right* people are!"

Even if you are not currently in a position to make hiring decisions, self-evaluation is always healthy. In times of crisis, when many companies are forced to consider cutting back, you want to be the last person considered for elimination. Your chances of success are much improved in your current position if you develop the qualities described in this chapter. You literally become the "best of breed." Whether you are looking for a job or desire a promotion, these qualities will make you a better employee and improve your options. If you are in a position where you select your own team, these principles are mandatory for the release of your CEO within.

No one who is hired from outside an organization can possibly be as well known to management as an internal candidate. It follows that training, developing, and refining the skills of all associates is a well-placed investment. The growth and evolution of an organization eventually requires new skills that are not currently present, and this makes advancing an in-house associate impractical. Therefore, external recruitment, which is more difficult, becomes necessary. Unfortunately, external recruitment leads to higher turnover. Specific skills must be developed in order to increase your organization's batting average whether promoting from within or recruiting externally.

Many experts say the 80/20 rule is a good guideline—80 percent of promotions should be internal and 20 percent should be from external sources. This is mainly food for thought as no absolutes can be applied. The benefits of external hires include preventing a company from becoming too narrow in its thinking and promoting change within the company. These are positive results that encourage diversity. Diversity of thinking and experience is of great value to a company. Diversity as related to gender, race, creed, or ethnic background does not automatically provide these values.

For a very long time, our company was focused on internal promotion, and we became narrow in our thinking. We saw promotion as a major incentive for our employees and neglected to see the benefits of external hires. We anticipated our employees' desire for opportunity and advancement, and we wanted to avoid the fallout of unwanted turnover. How would those who saw the best jobs going to external hires think they would ever get ahead by staying with us? We wanted to encourage our present employees with promotions, and we invested heavily in developmental programs—especially for those with high potential.

What better guidelines for building a team exist than those given in God's Word? The Scriptural instruction for placing someone in one of the highest positions in the church basically says they should be tried and investigated and proved first, and if they turn out to be above reproach then and only then should they be hired. "Let these also first be proved; then let them use the office of a deacon, being found blameless" (I Timothy 3:10 KJV).

Consulting the Bible for guidance in this important issue of hiring or promoting is the place to start. There are many Biblical illustrations of the need for organization and leaders. In the early history of the nation of Israel, Moses had overwhelming responsibilities. Jethro, Moses' father-in-law, observed Moses' efforts and advised him to organize and delegate. It was impossible for one man to do all that was required in executing his responsibilities and deciding the many cases that came before him. This same thing is true for any growing organization today.

Jethro gave Moses good advice. He not only gave organizational ideas but also the qualifications of those who would fill the newly formed positions: "Select capable men from all the people—men who fear God, trustworthy men who hate dishonest gain—and appoint them as officials over thousands, hundreds, fifties and tens." (Exodus 18:21 NIV)

The ideal candidate for any job should meet these qualifications first: God-fearing, honest, and trustworthy. In hiring and promoting, start with the ideal; the Scriptural design is just that. Notice the emphasis on competence ("capable") and character ("trustworthy, hate dishonest gain").

The fundamental component in selecting capable and trustworthy men and women is the comparison of the candidate's qualifications to those of an overseer, found in I Timothy 3:1-7. "Overseer" is the term used in Scripture for a leader or manager. Please notice that 8 of these 11 most desirable qualities relate primarily to character:

- Conduct above reproach
- Not promiscuous
- Self-controlled, temperate
- Dignified, orderly, and disciplined
- Hospitable
- A good teacher
- Not given to strong drink
- Not greedy for money
- Has excellent family relationships
- Must not be inexperienced for the job
- A good reputation outside the business world

The objective is to hire highly qualified entry-level employees, those who seem likely to grow and have the potential to become an overseer. Don't become disillusioned when finding that perfect individual proves difficult. Better to aim for the moon and hit the ceiling than never to aim and not get off the floor!

The first step in the process of reproducing is preparation. Define the job clearly and create the profile of the ideal candidate. This profile should include the most desired qualities, education, experience, and technical knowledge. Invest the necessary time and research in drafting this important document. Effective planning is important in all business endeavors, and the selection of your team is no exception.

There is a logical progression in this selection process, and each step depends on satisfactorily completing the previous one.

1. Develop sources of applicants.
2. Conduct initial interviews (a telephone interview is a prerequisite).
3. Conduct an in-depth interview (allow plenty of time).
4. Conduct testing.
5. Check references and conduct background checks.
6. Others from both inside and outside the organization interview the candidate.
7. Conduct the final interview and present the offer.

The candidate you are seeking is well described in Proverbs 22:29, "Do you see a man who excels in his work? He will stand before kings; he will not stand before unknown men."

Begin developing sources for applicants with a look at your current associates. After searching diligently for a VP of Human Resources, we selected a current employee who had little HR experience, but was well known, respected in the company, and also had a wealth of business experience. She rapidly developed and became an excellent HR executive.

When recruiting from without, there are several sources that may be used. Display advertisements in the newspaper are still effective. Make them large with a border so they stand out. Place the ads in the financial or sports section of the local newspaper. Search firms are a good source and will do a good job if you invest time to familiarize them with your business, the job requirements, and your goals and vision for the operation. College campus recruiting is also a wonderful source for many jobs and specialties. The most contemporary source—the Internet—is extremely useful. There are many sites for posting jobs and searching for applicants, such as Monster.com. Current employees are always a valuable source for finding new employees. An employee should receive a finder's fee when the person they recommend is hired.

All of these sources can be used effectively; match the source to the job category.

Determine to hire the best person for the job. Patience and diligence are required. Reach your final decision based on facts and not on "shoot from the hip" emotional conclusions. Prepare to spend lots of time with the candidate. Look for certain characteristics of an applicant that determine continuing interviews. Don't go further and waste your candidate's time or your own if you see a "knockout factor." An early knockout factor is a candidate's frequent job changes. This is a warning flag. There is the strong possibility that the candidate will continue this behavior at your expense.

Design creative questions to learn why the candidate changed jobs. If he says, "I didn't like my boss," does it mean the candidate changed jobs to avoid authority? Also, ask questions about his relationship with co-workers. If an employee has never liked any boss and does not get along well with co-workers, you have the needed information. On the other hand, there may be credible reasons for frequent job changes such as moving to a better job, promotions, higher pay, etc. The quality you are seeking is loyalty. Be sensitive to a humble spirit in a candidate. Humility goes hand in hand with loyalty. The early use of creative questions will determine if you should continue with this applicant.

We frequently asked the question, "Would you like to be in business for yourself?" This question is a two-sided coin. On the one hand, after you invest in their training and they become more productive, they might leave to begin their own business. On the other hand, you admire and know the value of their entrepreneurial spirit. Likely, they will work on their own without direct supervision and will respond strongly to incentives. Although difficult, the interviewer must make a judgment based on the response and discern the motive of the candidate.

Whether a candidate is being considered for hiring or promotion, look for a pattern of success. Did the candidate do well in everything they attempted, and did they complete—finish the job? This is particularly true of college, did they finish what they started? The candidate's college record is important. How did the candidate perform academically? Some students do well because they are gifted; it's easy for them. Others do well because they work hard. Experts tell us that the test that most frequently correlates with success is mental ability, but this is of little value without a good work ethic. Intelligence combined with diligence will produce outstanding results.

> *"When you hire people that are smarter than you are,*
> *you prove you are smarter than they are."*
> *-R. H. Grant*

The intent behind the anti-discrimination laws is good, but it can be cumbersome in getting to the truth regarding a candidate. Creativity is required in order to get all the facts without violating any laws. Testing is difficult because of the fact that some tests are racially biased and don't pass the discrimination test. You will find tests that have been validated for your industry. The best test is one that simulates actually doing the job, and these are always valid.

You can develop an appropriate test for a particular job. For example, our sales reps had to be able to load and unload a copier from a van, which required physical strength. For those who applied for sales jobs, we simply had them try the loading/unloading procedure. This was an on-the-job test that was automatically validated.

The technical competence required for a particular job may be difficult to determine if you do not have work experience or education in that field. For example, when I was interviewing for a research and development manager, I had limited experience in this field. In such cases, involve someone else who thoroughly understands the process and technology to interview the applicant. Multiple interviews conducted by different people with no personal stake in the outcome are extremely helpful. This is a Biblical principle at work: "Where there is no counsel, the people fall; but in the multitude of counselors there is safety." (Proverbs 11:14)

Be especially alert for character issues. How can we discern the character of another person? King Solomon, the wisest man in the world, wrote about the things that the Lord hates. Be alert to these qualities and avoid such a person: "These six [things] the LORD hates, yes, seven are an abomination to Him: a proud look, a lying tongue, hands that shed innocent blood, a heart that devises wicked plans, feet that are swift in running to evil, a false witness who speaks lies, and one who sows discord among brethren." (Proverbs 6:16-19)

A great line of questioning to discover character might be phrased like this: "Has there ever been a time in your life when you took a stand that was unpopular? Has there been a time when you stood alone in defending someone or some idea? What would you describe as the defining moment of your life?" The depth of answers to these questions will provide great insight into the character of anyone. All applicants will speak highly of themselves as we learn from Proverbs 20:6: "Most men will proclaim each his own goodness, but who can find a faithful man?"

Look for any hint of deception in a prospective employee. Overstating educational background and professional experience is incredibly common, and a thorough professional background check will uncover these facts. It is a legal requirement that you have the applicant's permission to order such a report. The report should verify educational experience and determine if there have been felony convictions. Long periods of self-employment are difficult to check, but you must find a way. Time unaccounted for can be used to cover illegal entanglements or other activities that indicate a lack of desired character. The research available on the Internet is invaluable. Many sources are available to you online with just a few clicks, but always double check all such information.

The honesty and integrity of an individual will be exposed in their written records, application, and job history. Discovering misstatements or misleading information is definitely a strong caution. You are at a point of decision. You must decide to continue beyond these cautions and other unexplained inconsistencies or stop the process immediately.

Every job the candidate has held for the last 15 years should be verified. When investigating previous employment, human resources departments are cautious and will provide only verification of employment and salary information. Be sure to ask, "Would this person be eligible for rehire?" A negative response is a red flag.

The most fail-safe procedure is to arrange a private conversation with someone in the organization who directly supervised the candidate.

Although it will require personal time, you should pursue that important contact and information. Do not trust this final confirmation to your human resources staff or a placement firm.

At one time I was seeking an experienced administrative assistant. There was a highly qualified candidate, and in the final process, I personally began to check her references. According to her application, she had previously served as an assistant to a CEO in Houston. In a private telephone conversation, I learned that he didn't even know her. She had worked for his company—but not for him. This phone call prevented a costly mistake. Confirmation of the applicant's previous work experience is extremely important.

We routinely hired sales reps and there was a lot of turnover in our company. Gene was upset about the turnover and scheduled a industrial psychologist to conduct a training session. He taught us many techniques for questioning and getting to the truth. He talked about detecting patterns of success in our recruits. But then he made a memorable statement that astounded me. He said, "People never change except when one of these three events takes place in their lives: (1) frontal lobotomy, (2) deep psychiatric therapy, or (3) a religious experience." Unless you're prepared to guarantee that you can make one or more of these three events happen, you'll have to hire people with a successful work history. When the psychologist finished, Gene made the sarcastic comment regarding our offices, "It appears to me that we are running 141 rehabilitation centers across the nation."

Coming from a secular background, the psychologist surprised me with his reference to a "religious experience". As a Christian I knew exactly what he meant. Saul, a persecutor and murderer of Christians was radically changed when he met Jesus. His name was changed and Paul became a major factor in establishing the church. Chuck Colson, a leader of the "dirty tricks" operation in the Nixon Administration came to know Jesus and was radically changed. He founded a very effective evangelistic prison ministry. It has been said "If your religion hasn't changed you, you should change your religion." Those who receive Jesus know it is not religion but relationship with Him that changes anyone. (John 1:12)

No matter what you may have done in the past, if you confess your sin and turn your life over to Jesus you will be forever changed. Even with radical change in your behavior, it will take time to re-establish your reputation. We are told "let them be proven". (I Timothy 3:10) On the flipside, the same applies when hiring someone with a questionable background who has recently become a Christian. Time is required in order to re-establish and validate that radical change has occurred and behavior has changed.

Unfortunately, people don't often change. Determining the candidate's past gives you a clearer picture of your future with them. Many arrogant leaders believe they can rehabilitate those with questionable backgrounds. If you think you can correct previous problems and rehabilitate poor applicants, you'll get shot down in flames before you can develop your skill of reproducing. You must never hire based on the possibility of a change in character. Character demonstrated in the past will continue.

Would hiring only Christians solve the problem of determining the character of your applicant? Of course, we readily know that to do so except in a religious organization would be illegal. Therefore, you are not free to inquire. Besides, hiring only Christians wouldn't solve the problem of character. Unfortunately, the evidence indicates that those who profess to be Christians do not perform any better that those who do not. In general, professing Christian employees are just as much trouble as non-Christians. My friend Larry Burkett of Christian Financial Concepts stated that even though he attempted to hire all Christians for his ministry organization, the problems remained similar to those he had faced in the secular workplace

My wife once said to me after several home improvement projects, "I'm looking for a competent pagan contractor." She had been disappointed with the carelessness and deception of several so-called Christian men who had worked on projects at our home. Broken promises, unfair charges, and other such character flaws were the issues that elicited her cynical statement.

Many Christians use the Scripture regarding not being unequally yoked (II Corinthians 6:14) as their reason for hiring only Christians. However, the yoke relationship does not apply to the relationship of a business owner and an employee. In the yoke analogy, the oxen are made to work in unison mechanically. If one falls, so does the other. If one pulls and the other doesn't, both fail. If one turns left, so does the other. The weight must be equally distributed and borne by both.

The yoke relationship is analogous to business partnerships and equal ownerships. Partnerships are dangerous from many aspects, but the most dangerous situation is when it's not clear who's in charge. Someone must have the final authority, and for this to work well, someone must be the majority owner.

If hiring only Christians were the answer, there are simply not enough Christians to fill all the openings. More importantly, we miss one of the greatest opportunities for evangelism that we will experience in our entire life—hiring the competent, reliable, lost person of good character.

In I Corinthians 5:9-10, Paul states, "I have written you in my letter not to associate with sexually immoral people—not at all meaning the people of this world who are immoral, or the greedy and swindlers, or idolaters. In that case you would have to leave this world." (NIV) Our work is in the world. Christ desires to reveal Himself in the context of our work. We cannot altogether shun the immoral people of the world since this would require that we get out of the marketplace, the world, and human society.

In my first management job, hiring was a major part of my responsibility. I was in the process of developing my skills of reproducing—multiplying our sales and service operations in order to produce outstanding results. As I became more and more aware that God had a purpose in my business, I prayed about each decision, particularly when hiring and promoting.

For some time we had no sales rep in Lake Charles. The area was a good market that we were covering for service only, an untapped potential. The task of hiring a sales representative was before me, and I prayed diligently in preparation for the interviews. A large display ad (not in the classified section) was placed in the local paper. To avoid interruptions, I received the calls in my hotel room. The results were disappointing. There were few calls.

At the end of the day I had eliminated all those who responded to the ad except for one candidate. I was discouraged and uncomfortable with the odds. This one and only applicant had great sales experience, a college education, and few job changes. He was married with several children, and all his information seemed fine. I liked everything I had learned up to this point in the process and we made an appointment for the preliminary interview.

The applicant arrived well-dressed and handled himself quite well. We sat down to talk; he was easy to talk to and especially likable. Since I had actually been a salesman, I could easily discern that this man knew how to sell.

One of the questions we always asked was, "Have you ever been arrested." I was shocked when he answered, "Yes!" Naturally, I asked some follow-up questions. He had been arrested in Lake Charles under a local ordinance called the "Green River Law." It was named for the city that first made a city ordinance against calling on someone in their home without an appointment. During his experience as an encyclopedia sales rep, cold calling was a way of life. He didn't know about the law and was aggressively doing his job. This struck me as humorous and also convinced me that this man had the courage and the persistence to do the tough things that make a great sales rep. And he had the notoriety of being arrested for doing his job!

There was one troubling concern. My prospective salesman had ruddy complexion and something about his eyes made me question if he was a heavy drinker. I immediately ordered a background check from a reliable professional company that specialized in such investigations, and I requested a rush. They confirmed within a few days that his education and all the other pertinent details were accurate. Interviewing his friends and associates determined that he did not drink at all. I was relieved and pleased with that good report.

As I proceeded to the next step of talking with his former employers, I was encouraged again. The employer with the encyclopedia company said, "If that guy is available, I'm going to do everything I can to hire him back and I want you to know that right now!"

Everything checked out well; I was elated. I recalled my initial disappointment that there was only one applicant. Then it dawned on me; God had answered my prayer. There only needed to be one—the one He sent.

My prospective salesman came on board and was an immediate success. He knew how to sell. My only responsibility was to teach him the products and the paperwork. Since he had a background in education, he was extremely helpful in selling to schools throughout Louisiana. The government had passed the Elementary and Secondary Education Act, and millions of dollars were available for schools to buy projectors and a multitude of other products we had in our line. Through his leadership, we hit the jackpot.

It only takes a few good hires to produce remarkable results. This one hire made a huge difference in the Baton Rouge district, and shortly after that year, I was promoted to one of the general management positions at headquarters. This one hire greatly accelerated my release. In only a few years, this sales rep was promoted to a high level position in the company. He won numerous sales contests and award trips on his way up.

Earlier I said we should consider every hire as a life or death situation. When hiring pilots, that was literally true. But one great individual added to an operation can bring new life. That is what Cecil did for us in Louisiana. The KEY of reproducing, hiring, and promoting high-quality, long-term associates is a requirement for release of your CEO within!

In the KEY of Reproducing, the following are the most important things to remember:

- Hire/promote those who have been successful in the past.
- Hire based on past performance, not on plans to rehabilitate.
- Check out the prospect's background thoroughly—turn over every rock.
- Check references personally—get to a supervisor with personal knowledge.
- Don't rush the process—complete every step.
- Pray diligently.

> *"Hire people who are better than you are, then leave them to get on with it . . . . Look for people who will aim for the remarkable, who will not settle for the routine."*
> —*David Ogilvy*

Chapter Six

The Key of Removing

Dealing with poor performance

He was, tall, attractive, and instantly likable. He was talented and a confident talker with a great sense of humor. These are attributes of most great salesmen. Hal's background was solid, but selling was a career change for him. I decided to take a chance on him.

Within a short length of time, it became evident that Hal had a personal discipline problem. He frequently arrived late for work, often offering lame excuses. One morning he explained that his wife had driven into the drugstore. I thought he meant she went to pick up a prescription, but he explained that she had poor eyesight and had literally "driven into the store" through the front plate-glass window. This was no lame excuse—it actually happened!

Even though Hal was talented, his work habits and lack of self discipline were counterproductive. The uncomfortable decision could no longer be delayed, we had to dismiss him.

I explained to Hal that he needed to find another job, one that was more structured and where his talents could be used, a new beginning for him—another new start. He was disappointed but receptive to my suggestion that he seek a different vocation. We parted as friends.

Years later, I returned to Baton Rouge to call on customers with sales and service reps. One of our sales rep asked me to accompany him to the State Department of Hospitals. The new charity hospital in Baton Rouge was under construction, and we were seeking the order for the dictation system. All the procurement for the new hospital had been assigned to a team of purchasing agents. Our objective was to meet with the head of the team and get our system specified.

Just imagine my surprise when we walked into the office and were introduced to the agent in charge. It was Hal! My immediate thought: "Oh my, that's the guy I fired!" Thankfully, he remembered my helpful suggestions instead. He expressed respect for the company and was receptive to our ideas for the dictation system. A few months later, we received the order.

In building a great organization, we must remove those who cannot or will not produce. Sometimes dismissal is based on lack of skills and talents required by the job; sometimes it is based on poor character or disloyalty.

This has been the most difficult part of this book for me to write. Removal is hard but necessary. No doubt this is the most uncomfortable part of any vocation, but it must be done or the organization can be severely handicapped. It could be the turning point of the operation as it was for me in my first management position.

When a new employee has been hired, there is always a trial period—whether it is formalized or not. With all positions, it is wise to establish benchmarks for achievement during the trial period, things you are looking for to ensure employee success. For administrative jobs we used a "temp to perm" concept. We hired temporary employees through an agency with the understanding that they would be transferred to permanent status within three months based on acceptable performance. This eliminated the legal issues that can often accompany dismissals.

In sales jobs, productivity quickly becomes apparent. The best definition of a salesman is "one who sells." Often a sales rep who is paid largely on commission will voluntarily resign when it is certain that sales productivity is short of producing an acceptable income.

There is a considerable amount of unwise thinking in the Christian community. Some believe that it is a poor witness for a Christian employer fire anyone. Some employees believe a Christian boss will never fire them—leading to lifetime employment regardless of performance. Such an arrangement will always result in abuse of the organization.

Businesspeople often say, "People are our most valuable asset." Improper management conduct makes it difficult for employees to believe this is true. When a good employee observes others who are undependable, incompetent, tardy, and don't obey policies being kept on the payroll, it says just the opposite. Keeping nonperforming employees puts more pressure on good performers. Keeping and developing high-performance employees sends the right message: "The <u>right</u> people are our most valuable asset."

The Biblical model for firing an employee is church discipline. The purpose of church discipline is restoring the errant member to full fellowship. In any organization, the first goal is to restore an employee to productivity. After training, discussion, and careful consideration prove ineffective, removal is the only answer. As in church discipline, dismissal is not done to destroy a person's life, but it is a last resort of correction. Throughout the process, leaders should keep an attitude of restoration for the individual, rather than becoming belligerent or vindictive. We should be willing to assist in finding a job with another company where the one being dismissed can be productive and happy. Here's the Scriptural process that is the model for removal: "If your brother sins against you, go and tell him his fault between you and him alone. If he hears you, you have gained your brother. But if he will not hear, take with you one or two more, that by the mouth of two or three witnesses every word may be established. And if he refuses to hear them, tell it to the church. But if he refuses even to hear the church, let him be to you like a heathen and a tax collector." (Matthew 18:15-17)

"Getting fired is nature's way of telling you that you had the wrong job in the first place."
—*Hal Lancaster, Wall Street Journal*

Fundamental steps must be completed before considering dismissing an employee.

- There must be a detailed job description.
- Requirements must be clearly stated.
- Expectations must be communicated in writing.
- Dissatisfaction with performance must be communicated immediately in writing. (Matthew 15:15)
- There must be a trial correction period.

Communication can be difficult even in pleasant circumstances. When faced with expressing dissatisfaction with another person, we can be hindered by concerns of hurting someone or causing others to not like us. We might even have a mistaken idea about our Christian witness being damaged. Scripture states that our speech is to be straightforward, clear, sticking with our decision; in other words, there is no room for misunderstanding or confusion. "Above all, my brethren, do not swear, either by heaven or by earth or with any other oath. But let your 'Yes' be 'Yes,' and your 'No,' 'No,' lest you fall into judgment." (James 5:12)

In my early management experience I was often overly kind and softened my corrective comments. In a management course I learned of the so-called "sandwich approach": Sandwich the bad news between two compliments to soften the message and make it less offensive. Unfortunately, this method dilutes the purpose of the communication, and in most cases the recipient only remembers the good things they heard. The sandwich approach can also cause confusion. An employee may not trust your genuine compliments nor recognize useful constructive criticism. We must be sure that the message of unsatisfactory performance is heard and understood. Later, I discovered the benefit of clear communication and the dreadful cost of not doing so.

Regular scheduled meetings with each employee to review job performance are invaluable. During these meetings, review the requirements of their job. Repeating these requirements simply reinforces their importance in the employee's mind. Discuss any performance issues and be sure the employee understands fully. If there is a problem that could lead to dismissal, rehearse and perhaps review with someone else to be sure you are well prepared. Record the problems or issues in written format, and place the document in the employee's hands with duplicates in their file. Even if the employee does not agree with the issues, secure their signature as an acknowledgment that they have received the warning.

Words of correction are often not heeded. Proverbs 29:19 warns, "A servant will not be corrected by mere words; for though he understands, he will not respond." Carefully analyze each situation. Mistreatment of an employee may cause them to retreat and not respond. An employee who is lazy and has slothful motives may not respond. You will have to draw the person out to truthfully communicate and determine the situation.

It is wise to have a witness present when dealing with difficult issues. Select someone in a neutral management position. This is particularly helpful if the employee is prone to emotional outbursts. Guard against your own anger and emotional responses. You must not make statements you will later regret. Remember, "A man without self-control is like a city broken into and left without walls." (Proverbs 25:28 ESV)

Time will not make awkward, difficult situations better. Deal with employee problems immediately. Delay in doing so will only allow bad circumstances to get worse. "It takes only one wrong person among you to infect all the others—a little yeast spreads quickly through the whole batch of dough!" (Galatians 5:9 NLT) When we allow a thief, dissenter, or slacker to continue uncorrected, it will encourage this behavior on the part of others.

There are several justifiable reasons for firing an employee.

Dishonesty

When dishonesty is tolerated or overlooked, the crooked prosper and the honest suffer. "He who walks in his uprightness fears the LORD, but he who is perverse in his ways despises Him." (Proverbs 14:2)

Several years ago, through a routine audit, we discovered that used copiers were missing in one of our offices. We discovered that the district manager was selling this equipment to a used equipment dealer for cash and personally pocketing the money. Naturally, our policy required that all equipment be accounted for and that all sales be approved and handled by the headquarters office. The dealer shared the information with us; he was unaware that we were not receiving the money.

The guilty district manager ran one of the highest performing offices in the company. We were concerned about firing such a productive manager who otherwise had an excellent record. We agreed that we would keep him with the company only if he was repentant and agreed to pay back what he had taken. In addition, he would be demoted to a lower level job. When confronted, he became angry, defensive, and simply said everyone else in the company was doing it. Based on his response we had to terminate him.

Even if a dishonest employee is repentant and willing to make restitution, you take a big risk in keeping them in the company. Their good reputation must be re-established (earned), and this takes time. Let them re-establish with someone else. Dismissing a dishonest employee will greatly improve your odds of success. When word gets around, other employees will not be tempted to steal from the company. It is leadership's responsibility to establish policies that encourage honesty and remove temptations to be dishonest.

According to a *Wall Street Journal* article, fraud is growing rapidly in small businesses. Some companies go out of business not even realizing that their demise was due to employee fraud. The article, "Small Businesses Face More Fraud in Downturn" claims that fraud is harder to detect because of a high degree of trust between employers and employees in a small business. Ronald Reagan's motto was, "trust, but verify!"

One responsibility of leadership is to remove temptations for dishonesty as much as possible. Weigh the possibilities carefully when considering whether to bring formal charges against a dishonest employee. If the theft is a nominal amount and dismissal from their job seems adequate, you might choose not to bring formal charges. However, when you press formal charges, it makes a dramatic statement to other employees. This will be a decision made on a case-by-case basis. Ephesians 4:28 reminds us of the alternative for stealing: "Let him who stole steal no longer, but rather let him labor, working with his hands what is good, that he may have something to give him who has need."

Another expression of dishonestly is bearing false witness: lying to the boss, lying to customers, lying to fellow employees. In many cases lying is costly to the company, and the net effect is just like stealing money or goods. Sometimes sales reps promise things to customers that are not in the contract. The company must keep the promise even though the customer did not pay for it. These "extras" must be charged to the sales rep's commission account. In addition, the rep must be given a warning, and if it continues, termination would be required.

Training and policy orientation must be emphasized or much abuse will occur.

Disobedience

In Bible times, the master/slave relationship was the best depiction of the boss/employee relationship as expressed in the culture of that day. We are to obey all authorities appointed over us. Titus 2:9 states, "Slaves are to be submissive to their own masters in everything; they are to be well-pleasing, not argumentative." (ESV) There are many degrees of disobedience, ranging from outright rebellion to subtle areas of disloyalty. Outright rebellion is easy to deal with—either it stops immediately or the employee is dismissed. However, subtle disobedience is just that, subtle. Being sensitive in the little things becomes very important. Disobedience equates to disloyalty. Disloyalty must be dealt with or it will destroy any organization.

When instructions are not followed completely, we must determine if disloyalty is brewing. Actively disloyal people are shrewd and difficult to catch in the act. Do not make the mistake of ascribing disloyalty to those with new and creative ideas. All employees should be encouraged to present their ideas. We stifle creativity when we do not allow improved ideas that differ from our own to be openly expressed and implemented. You'll be amazed at the improvements that result from having a teachable attitude and an eye for new methods. Nothing cramps any organization's progress more than "we've always done it this way."

Laziness

The Bible refers to laziness as slothfulness and condemns this behavior in more than 20 verses. For example, "He who is slothful in his work is a brother to him who is a great destroyer." (Proverbs 18:9) Also, "Because of laziness the building decays, and through idleness of hands the house leaks." (Ecclesiastes 10:18) The mark of laziness is a lack of productivity. Slothful people are not punctual, take too many breaks, and offer many excuses—phrases like "the dog ate my homework" come to mind. Many sloths spend more time explaining away the obvious than they spend actually working. One pastor said that an excuse is a lie wrapped in the skin of a reason. The answer to this problem is simple. Set minimum productivity standards.

Provide adequate training, emphasizing standards that must be met on a consistent basis. If standards are not being met after providing a warning, it is time to dismiss this employee.

Incompetence

Perhaps the most difficult situation is when an employee is motivated and cooperative, but is incompetent—he or she simply cannot do the job, or lacks mental or physical ability. You cannot correct this problem. Transferring the employee to a different job more suited to their abilities or dismissal of the employee are the only solutions.

In some cases, job requirements change and the employee becomes incompetent based on changes in the business. This can happen to anyone in any position. Each employee is personally responsible for continuing to study and learn more about their job, which is always evolving. We must be conscientious to "study to [show] thyself approved unto God, a workman that needeth not to be ashamed, rightly dividing the word of truth." (II Timothy 2:15 KJV) Just we are admonished to study the Word, we must study and keep up with our profession or we will fall behind and become obsolete. This will require effort on our own time although many companies will offer training programs. Today's technology changes so quickly and requires lifelong learning in every job. Some jobs are even eliminated with new systems and process changes. Anticipate change and be ready to embrace it. We are each responsible to stay competent for the task ahead.

Unwilling to change

Once a termination decision has been made, a trial correction period should take place, giving the employee an opportunity to change. Determine a specific length of time for the trial period and explain the exact purpose for the trial to the employee, providing the minimum requirements in writing. Copies of this document should be kept in the employee's file.

During the trial period, hold regular, face-to-face follow-up meetings. The employee should always be informed of where they stand and given adequate opportunity to make corrections. Documentation of all meetings provides great protection from lawsuits filed by those who have been dismissed. With adequate documentation, you can virtually eliminate all EEOC complaints and avoid legal entanglements.

When an employee has been terminated, promptly conduct an exit interview. Such an interview may reveal what went wrong. Corrections can then be made, whether it is in hiring procedures or in company policy. The employee should leave the premises as soon as possible. Every effort should be made to protect the dignity of the employee, including adequate severance pay and referrals if there are no character problems. Remember that many people who fail at one job do very well at another.

Although Christians tend to err by keeping poor employees too long, there are a few cases where the decision to terminate should be aborted. If the correction period brings desirable results, then keep the employee. Careful supervision is necessary to assure that the changes are long-lasting and not just temporary performance under pressure. When an employee genuinely wants to change for the better, provide an adequate opportunity to prove that the change in conduct is genuine.

Some employees are difficult and unlikable, yet they are competent. Something about them might simply rub you the wrong way. Perhaps they point out flaws in the plan you have conceived. Even when their suggestions are right, you may struggle with receiving them. If there are no character problems, this employee may have been placed by the Lord to smooth some rough spots in your management style. Perhaps the Lord has sent someone to be "heavenly sandpaper" in your life. If you find yourself struggling with someone's behavior, remember that this could be revelation of your own character. The Scripture points out that when we judge the behavior of others, we may have the same issues in our own behavior. "You are inexcusable, O man, whoever you are who judge, for in whatever you judge another you condemn yourself; for you who judge practice the same things." (Romans 2:1)

Prevention is the best answer to the problem of removing. Adequate testing and background checks are your first line of defense. However in entry-level jobs, where the employee is hired to learn how to do the job, it is difficult to determine their capacity to perform beforehand. If and when a mistake is made, correct it quickly before the damage spreads.

Reflecting on my first management assignment, it would have been a great help to know what I'm writing about now. When I arrived in Baton Rouge, the top salesman in the entire company was working in that office. He was a smart Cajun with a propensity for deception. We had met previously on an incentive trip. Even on a pleasure trip, we had a heated argument. His position was that you had to lie in order to sell the product. When I became his boss, I knew that we could clash on this issue.

As I struggled with learning all the new skills required to be a good district manager, I was under intense pressure. It seemed that some unseen force hindered everything I attempted. I had hired several new sales reps, and some of them were doing quite well. While making sales calls with one of the new reps, he confided to me that the top salesman, Mike (not his real name), was undermining everything I attempted to do. After each meeting I had with the employees, Mike would take everyone to a local bar and explain why everything I had said was wrong. Since he was tops in the company most everyone listened to him. They thought it likely I wouldn't be there much longer. Since my confidant was new to the company, he saw Mike's motive was to get my job. Mike thought that being the company's top sales rep entitled him to the manager's job.

With this new understanding of the underlying issue, I decided I must confront Mike. I invited him to my home so that we could have a private conversation. When I told him what I knew, he expressed remorse and promised that his behavior would change. He even shed tears, and I thought the problem was over. This was my first experience with counterfeit repentance, but it was not the last. Mike was not out the door before his propensity for deception continued. He wanted to save his job, but he was not willing to change his behavior.

After experiencing firsthand the devastating effects of Mike's disloyalty and then receiving confirmation in a management development program that I described previously, I decided that I must get him out of the company. But my lingering thought was, "What will my boss think about my firing the top sales rep in the company?"

My decision was final. I had confronted Mike, and the behavior continued. My only choice was to take action or face the consequences. Carefully, I planned our final interview. Since Mike had such a perverse impact on the entire organization, I knew the "end of the story" had to be an impressive conclusion.

Mike had won the annual sales incentive trip and returned to the office on Monday morning bragging about his trip to New York. He had his latest trophy and proudly placed it on his desk. Summoning him to my office, I informed him that this was his last day with the company. After confiscating his keys, I directed him to immediately gather all his personal possessions and leave the office. He was shocked and unbelieving as he stormed out of the office. Everyone saw him leave and knew that something significant had happened.

Immediately I called an impromptu meeting with all the employees. I explained the incident and why such disloyal behavior would not be tolerated. All the sales reps enthusiastically participated in re-allocating sales territories—an enhanced opportunity for each of them. Mike had attempted to control such matters in the past because he wanted to keep the best for himself.

A wave of relief and excitement swept through the office. The resolution of this atmosphere of deception gave everyone certainty about who was in charge. They knew change was on their horizon. Even with a feeling of elation, the fear of my boss' reaction when he learned that I had fired the top sales rep in the company was hanging over me. A few days later, I received a call from Gene Milner. I was shaking in my boots as I picked up the phone. He immediately said, "I heard that you fired Mike. I always knew you would have to fire that $@&, but I knew you had to make this decision on your own. Today you became a man, my boy." I recalled Gene's rare confirmation many times through the years.

This one decision to remove this disloyal employee was the platform for our becoming the most productive office in Lanier. It's obvious that one detractor, even though personally productive, can negatively affect the performance of all others. Our revenue increased by 400 percent over the next three years, and I received my first big promotion.

You can't build a great team without talent. You can't build a great team with players who don't show up. You can't build a great team by tolerating poor performance. You can't build a great team by recruiting referees to play on your team. You can't build a great team without character. A great team requires wise recruiting or drafting. It requires practice and conditioning. It requires playing by the rules. And it requires making cuts.

Remember these major points:

- The Biblical purpose for separation is restoration.
- Job requirements must be clearly understood.
- Regular meetings with all those you supervise are required.
- Documentation is the key to removing without legal entanglement.
- Never tolerate dishonesty.
- Tolerating incompetence is deadly.
- Never tolerate disloyalty.

Without the KEY of Removing, I would have failed as a manager. In every business, there is the necessity to remove those who don't meet the requirements. It is one of the keys to releasing your CEO within!

A company that hires the right people and manages them properly does little firing, but releasing your mistakes is inevitable.
-Unknown

Chapter Seven

The Key of Resolving

Becoming a decisive leader

Corporate headquarters could be an intimidating place. Being there added a new element of anxiety; my feelings ranged from fear and rejection to occasional exhilaration. The chairman and his staff were meeting with and me and David Marini, General Manager of International Operations. The discussion around the conference table was focused on the largest acquisition in the history of our company. Besides being located in Europe, there were many other concerns and a number of unknowns about this potential acquisition.

In order to participate in the acquisition process, we had to meet the challenge of preparing a proposal to be presented to the selling organization and their investment bankers. Obviously, this would be an expensive endeavor. A team would travel to Brussels for the discovery process. Our rough estimate of the entry fee would be over $500,000 just to gather facts and prepare the proposal.

After a detailed discussion of the project we viewed as a great opportunity, the chairman said, "Wes, I am going to leave the decision on the proposal totally up to you. However, you should know that if you decide to go forward with the proposal, there is less than a 5-percent chance that I would ever approve this acquisition."

Those odds seemed overwhelming to everyone else sitting at the table. I could not control the smile that formed on this former salesman's face, and I felt David's excitement as he could barely contain himself either. I responded to the chairman, "Wow, those are the best odds I've ever experienced—we'll move ahead!" Everyone in the room, shocked at the exchange, burst into robust laughter.

Making effective decisions that resolve the many everyday issues in an organization is an absolute requirement for leadership. Making high-quality decisions and orchestrating their implementation is a key capability. No amount of hard work will make a wrong decision work properly. When a decision proves to be ineffective, the leader must set aside pride, unwind the damage, and move ahead by correcting the mistake quickly. Such prompt action is valuable to the ultimate outcome.

"Whenever you see a successful business, someone once made a courageous decision."
—*Peter Drucker*

How was I prepared to answer the chairman's challenge so quickly? What were the elements that enabled a quick and accurate decision against such overwhelming odds?

Gene, my former boss of 30 years was a tough, decisive man. He believed that any worthwhile decision should be made instantly. It was not difficult to see that I disappointed him because of my tendency to think about things too long—to study and even to sleep on many decisions. My boss's tendency to make many decisions quickly and emotionally often set him up for colossal mistakes. Yet he astounded us with how frequently he was right on target, especially when the company was small and less complicated.

My friend and mentor, Carl Reith, knew Gene quite well. He suggested that Gene was more concerned that I actually make a decision, and he was not as concerned with the speed of the process. Gene knew that a lack of decisiveness greatly hinders leadership, and indecisiveness slows the progress of the organization as it awaits leadership decisions. Carl suggested that I respond to Gene's requests by simply and candidly explaining that I would like time to gather information and would have my answer by a specific time. Gene's desire was that we not allow important decisions to linger unresolved, and he was definitely right about that.

> *"When you have to make a choice and you don't make it,*
> *that itself is a choice."*
> *—William James*

The opposite of decisiveness might be described as being double-minded or wavering to and fro, leaving all those who depend on you in an uncertain position. If you chase two rabbits, both will escape! Competitors could be gaining market share while you are being indecisive or taking too long in the process.

Life requires that we evaluate courses of action quickly and accurately. Without a doubt, this is essential in leadership. Great leaders have amazing foresight. They prepare for the future and avoid failures. In evaluating all circumstances, present and future, we must choose the best course of action. Sometimes we will be pressured by others to reconsider or change a decision that is based on a principle. We should defend our position with firmness when we know it is the right decision. By using a Biblical approach, a leader can be confident, emphatic, resolute, and certain about any decision.

> *"It's not hard to make decisions when you know*
> *what your values are."*
> *—Roy Disney*

There are those who actively resist any decision that involves change. When a decision is unpopular, implementation skills are as important as the decision itself. A decision that requires a major change in the status quo falls into this category. Making the decision may prove to be the easiest part. Meeting the challenge of implementation will emphatically demonstrate commitment to the decision.

All aspects of life require making decisions—many are irrevocable. For instance, based on the fact that the Lord hates divorce, the marriage decision must be approached as a permanent one. Great care and prayer should precede this important decision. Once the deal is done, you cannot unwind it without harm and destruction.

Putting God's perspective first would eliminate the need for many decisions. It is far better to prepare with His wisdom and prevent rather than repair and repent.

Major decisions are often the product of a series of little decisions that lead to the solution. There are principles in Scripture that provide five major considerations for making wise, effective decisions. When these five points are in alignment, the likelihood of success is greatly increased.

When landing an airplane on an aircraft carrier, the pilot visually lines up the aircraft with the landing deck and begins the descent. The carrier's signal officer closely observes and gives the pilot verbal as well as visual feedback on speed, rate of descent, glide path, and altitude—as well as attitude. If all these factors are in alignment, the plane lands safely. If one facet is doubtful, the plane is waved off. The pilot is in control, but he carefully considers each aspect before making the final decision. In the same fashion, the possibility of making a high-quality decision is much greater when all five considerations are in alignment. These considerations are: (1) conviction within, (2) confirmation of Scripture, (3) counsel of others, (4) common sense, and (5) circumstances without.

Any decision begins with **conviction within**. Christians often refer to this conviction as the "still, small voice" that gives us direction. Proverbs 2:6 states, "The LORD gives wisdom; from His mouth come knowledge and understanding." The Lord is the true Source of excellent decision making; wisdom comes only from Him. He gives us a sense of conviction that begins the process. Psalm 37:4-5 promises, "Delight yourself also in the LORD, and He shall give you the desires of your heart. Commit your way to the LORD, trust also in Him, and He shall bring it to pass." The Lord places desires in the heart of the one who truly delights in Him. When God is our heart's delight, then we will have our heart's desire. This Scripture is often misconstrued to say that He will give us whatever we want, but this is a confusion of the verse's meaning. The question is a straightforward one, "Am I truly delighting in Him?" In other words, am I choosing His ways and not my ways? Am I relying upon Him and not being dependent on myself?

Trusting Him to guide and lead is to be our focus, and "He will bring it to pass." He has not promised to gratify all the appetites of the body, but to grant the desires of the heart—all the cravings of the soul from a heart that is fully relying on Him. With His confirmation through the Word comes peace. Every decision should ultimately be underlined with His peace. "Let the peace of Christ rule in your hearts, to which indeed you were called in one body. And be thankful." (Colossians 3:15 ESV)

James 3:18 explains the benefits of peace: "The harvest of righteousness (of conformity to God's will in thought and deed) is [the fruit of the seed] sown in peace by those who work for and make peace [in themselves and in others, that peace which means concord, agreement, and harmony between individuals, with undisturbedness, in a peaceful mind free from fears and agitating passions and moral conflicts]." (AMP) It is as though the Lord is the continual and constant Umpire in our hearts. It is God's desire that we know His will. He wants us to know His will more than we want to know it.

Clearly the greatest tool in clarifying our conviction within is by the **confirmation of Scripture**. This should be our prayer, "For this reason we also, since the day we heard it, do not cease to pray for you, and to ask that you may be filled with the knowledge of His will in all wisdom and spiritual understanding." (Colossians 1:9) When we are filled with the knowledge of His will, making decisions is simple.

In the early days of Biblical history, God spoke directly to His chosen leaders. He spoke to Moses from a burning bush. Sometimes He spoke through appointed emissaries, such as angels. After the establishment of the Law, God spoke through priests, and they sought guidance through the use of the Urim and Thummim, a God-ordained method of casting lots. God sent prophets and spoke through them. Priests consulted the prophets for divine direction. Today we have the complete, revealed Word of God. In addition, we have the indwelling Holy Spirit who lives in each person who is born again. The written Word of God and the Living Word (Christ in us) will never contradict One another. We can totally depend upon the Word as our Source of guidance. We should be habitually reading, consulting, and committing His Word to memory.

With a working knowledge of the Word, decision making is simplified. When the Word gives absolute guidance, others' counsel and long hours of prayer are unnecessary. If the Word says it, that settles it.

One young man was seeking advice about marrying a certain young lady. He was instructed to search the Scriptures. After a few days, he foolishly reported, "Her name was not in there!" There are simply times when nothing is spelled out succinctly in the Word regarding the particular situation we are facing. Sometimes individuals approach the Word with a set answer already imprinted in their thinking. Often, they will find a verse or two which seems to support the decision they have already made. You must prayerfully come to the Word for direction. Approach the Scriptures "in neutral" with no preconceived or misconceived ideas in mind.

In regular reading and study of the Word, the Lord often will speak with a rhema, a Greek word which refers to a word that is spoken and means "an utterance." A rhema is a verse or portion of Scripture that the Holy Spirit brings to our attention with application to a current situation or need for direction. It is a personal Word from Him to you! The context, the setting—who, what, when, and where may in no way suit your situation, but the word of the Word speaks to your heart. You would not build your doctrinal beliefs upon that personal word taken out of context, but you could and should embrace the thought in application as He speaks it into your heart for direction in your present situation.

My wife and I were devastated when I received the diagnosis of prostate cancer. We were quick to call our family together for a time of sharing. The children offered words of encouragement and comfort and decided on a time for prayer and fasting. With the backdrop of their support, I studied the Word to learn what the Lord had to say about my situation. And there it was. What an astounding surprise. I was shocked that He answered so clearly. I could hardly believe it. I shared with Bernadine immediately, and she confirmed what I already knew—the Lord had spoken directly to me! God said to me through His Word: "You shall also know that your descendants shall be many, and your offspring like the grass of the earth. You shall come to the grave at a full age, as a sheaf of grain ripens in its season. Behold, this we have searched out; it is true. Hear it, and know for yourself." (Job 5:25-27)

Not only had this rhema been confirmed by numerous offspring (17 grandchildren at that time), but He said that I would not die until I was of full age. I would not die until the Lord deemed it the fullness of my season. (I have now lived 13 years since the diagnosis.) Best of all, it was for my good. We now have 22 grandchildren, and 2 great-grandchildren. I embraced the word the Lord gave me then, and this special encounter has prompted me to focus these sunset years of my life in service to His people through mentoring, teaching, testifying, and serving others. Yes, He wants us to know His will more than we want to know it!

Seeking the **counsel of others** is wise. Pride often prevents us from seeking counsel, and then pride keeps us from taking the advice. Consider what the book of Proverbs says about seeking counsel: "Where there is no counsel, the people fall; but in the multitude of counselors there is safety."(11:14) "Without counsel, plans go awry, but in the multitude of counselors they are established." (15:22) "Ointment and perfume delight the heart and the sweetness of a man's friend gives delight by hearty counsel." (27:9)

In all of life we need wise counselors. There is safety when we consult with several counselors. Selection of counselors in itself is an important step. Psalm 1:1a states, "Blessed is the man who walks not in the counsel of the ungodly." So how should we select our counselors?

The Lord knows the desires of our hearts, and if we are delighting in Him, He will lead us to Christian men and women who will give sound counsel. We can be confident that a person who is relying on the Word of God for personal direction and has a good reputation with their family will have something to offer in terms of wise counsel.

In *Business by the Book*, Larry Burkett suggests several questions you should ask yourself before seeking someone's counsel.

- Am I just looking for someone else to make the decision for me?

- Am I just shopping for rationalizations? This is a cognitive process of making something *seem* consistent with or based on reason. It could be an attempt to conceal your true motivation or a means of explaining your actions in a way that is not threatening. "The simple believes every word, but the prudent considers well his steps" (Proverbs 14:15).

- Am I looking for a miracle or a handout?

- Do I genuinely want counsel, or am I willing to accept advice that doesn't agree with my present direction?

Often, especially in the marketplace, we need professional counsel such as attorneys, accountants, compensation specialists, investment advisors, and marketing experts. The choice of whether to work only with Christians or the most competent secular counselors plagues the Christian in business. This question may even be prompted by the experience of receiving poor or bad advice from Christian professionals. When you have the authority to select counselors, always look for those with a Christian perspective and value system. Keep in mind, of course, that an incompetent Christian is still incompetent. An active discussion about values will provide the needed information. You must take the time to search and interview.

In some business situations, your authorities may provide counselors, and you will not be involved in the selection process. In that scenario, stick to your guns and offer your perspective. It's amazing how much agreement you can find on values, even with non-Christians.

Our authorities often have sound counsel to offer. Their experience can provide support and insight to improve the quality of decisions. God can "change the heart of the king," and He can certainly lead us through our authorities. Seeking your authority's counsel and guidance will sharpen your thought process, your reasoning, and your plan. Be cautious against asking your boss to make the decision for you. If your boss makes decisions for you, he or she will begin to wonder if you are necessary. High-level decisions will have to be approved by your manager or perhaps a board of directors. In this case you are not seeking counsel, but approval. The process you have followed to make the decision will lead to a persuasive presentation.

Wisdom applied to the problem might best be defined as **sanctified common sense**. The answers for many questions are intuitively obvious; however, selfishness and pride can blind us to the answer. Again, in seeking wise answers and making effective decisions, we must "decrease that He may increase" so that our thinking will be clear and not clouded. "God is not the author of confusion but of peace, as in all the churches of the saints . . . Let all things be done decently and in order." (I Corinthians 14:33, 40) Our thinking will be clear and not confused when we are listening to the Lord. Satan wants us to make poor decisions and will initiate confusion through the situation.

> *"Common sense suits itself to the ways of the world—*
> *Wisdom tries to conform to the ways of heaven."*
> —Joseph Joubert

In order to eliminate confusion, for many years I have used a common-sense tactic called the "Ben Franklin approach." On a piece of paper, I draw a vertical line down the middle. On the left, list favorable reasons for making a specific decision. On the right, list reasons against the decision. I've found this to be a useful tool because it provokes you to carefully consider each issue—pro and con. You must be sure to include insights from the other considerations. When you finish this exercise, the wisest decision usually becomes obvious. If you still cannot reach a firm decision, your counselors will prove helpful as they take a fresh look at your list.

Often a decision that seems intuitively right is totally wrong. As Scripture states, such decisions reached without considering the other guidelines leads to disaster: "There is a way that seems right to a man, but its end is the way of death." (Proverbs 14:12; 16:25)

Circumstances without, or external circumstances, should be the last consideration and are the least important of the aspects of making a wise decision. Circumstances should always be considered last. This is one area that Satan can counterfeit most readily, especially in the case of someone seeking a sign. Judges 6:37-40 speaks of asking for a sign, but we have our Sign, the Lord Jesus Christ. In the Old Testament, people did not have the entire revealed Word of God as we do today. By following the instructions we receive from the Word, from a rhema, and from the impression of the indwelling Holy Spirit, we will have to ignore conflicting circumstances.

Circumstances are often what lead us to making a decision in the first place. It is healthy to ask if the decision is needed and not be persuaded by external or competitive pressures. The enemy often uses circumstances to mislead, confuse, and thwart God's best for our lives.

In the early eighties, there was tremendous growth in the small-business computer market. Entering this business seemed natural to us because of our strong national sales force and customer-support organization. We made a decision to enter the market with a product called *Computereze*. It was a miserable failure because customers preferred open systems acquiring applications they wanted to run on a personal computer. Circumstances supported this decision, but it was a costly mistake.

The Scriptures give the clarification we need when considering circumstances. If we are fully yielded to His purpose and walking according to His calling on our life, all things will work for good. He will direct the decision. When God opens doors of opportunity, we should examine each one. We must have assurance that the opening is of the Lord. "I know your works. Behold, I have set before you an open door, which no one is able to shut. I know that you have but little power, and yet you have kept my word and have not denied my name." (Revelation 3:8 ESV)

Yes, the five considerations for making a wise decision can be in alignment, and you can go forth with confidence. The process will take time. However, it is far better to avoid a bad decision and having to unwind all its accompanying consequences.

Oh, yes, the rest of the acquisition story. After studying the data, our interest in the Agfa acquisition was now enhanced, but we knew that the competition was formidable. There were a couple of large public companies that would make aggressive bids. We felt sure that Credit Suisse-First Boston—skilled investment bankers who represented Agfa—would only consider the highest bid. Our Board of Directors voiced this same fear when I presented our plan for their approval. I suggested that Agfa might be more impressed with our commitment to customer satisfaction and our care for the Agfa associates we would employ. Our team did not see any way to increase our bid and still make our numbers work favorably. The Board approved our offer, but not one of them believed the bid would be successful.

Upon returning to my office and recognizing the reality that only a supernatural work of the Lord would make this deal come to fruition, I began to pray. A few days later, I attended a conference on prayer and fasting and took note of all the testimonies of miraculous answers to prayer. Immediately, I called the company leaders of the operating divisions. Upon my suggestion, they agreed to set aside a day for prayer and fasting. We asked the Lord for a miracle in the Agfa acquisition. We knew that with the difficult circumstances, only the Lord would receive credit for the outcome. There was no way one of us could make it happen. The odds were against us.

We prayed, we fasted, and we waited. Several weeks later, the word came! We were not the highest bidder, but Agfa thought we would take better care of the customers and their employees. Agfa declared us the successful bidder. It was a miracle of the Lord, and everyone knew it! This remains one of my most memorable miracles at Lanier. The guidelines for His guidance were used, and He made it happen.

One aspect that I must mention before closing this chapter on Resolving is that the greatest enemy of wise decision making is failing to wait on the Lord. "The LORD is good to those who wait for Him, to the soul who seeks Him." (Lamentations 3:25) Often the word *wait* is rejected without much thought. When we feel that we do not have direction, we choose to go ahead anyway rather than choosing to wait. To wait is not indecision; it is waiting for the wise answer, and He will make it clear "in His time"!

We should wait on the Lord and listen for His voice. When He speaks, we will recognize His voice. "When he brings out his own sheep, he goes before them; and the sheep follow him, for they know his voice." (John 10:4)

> *"Simply wait upon Him. So doing, we shall be directed, supplied, protected, corrected, and rewarded."*
> —*Vance Havner*

The KEY of Resolving is a major element in releasing your CEO within. Practice these Biblical guidelines for making effective decisions and you will be on the secure and certain pathway to becoming a decisive leader.

Chapter Eight

The Key of Reconciling

How to succeed at work without losing your family

It was past 8:30 p.m. as I opened the back door. I was late for dinner again. The atmosphere was thick, and I knew my wife was unhappy. I had failed to call her and I knew that she had waited with the four children as long as was practical. My dinner was cold and I sensed that her feelings were running hot. The children were in their pajamas waiting for their dad. My wife's irritation became more evident as she posed the questions, "Where were you? What were you doing?" Immediately, I felt that defensive tactic rising in my mind, but instead I attempted to explain.

One of our sales reps was in trouble in his marriage and I had spent more than an hour with him. I began my explanation, "I was giving Dave some marriage counseling!" The incredulous facial expression said enough, but she verbally added, "Oh great physician, heal thyself!"

One of my witty clichés has often been, "Even monkeys learn by repetition." I knew that this monkey was attending the school of learning. With many more experiences similar to this late appearance at home, I began to see that my pursuit of business success could be an enemy to my home life. My wrong choices were hurting my family life! ***There is no contentment at work when there is failure at home.***

The successful leadership and management of the family is an important qualification for the highest ranking offices in the church. "He must manage his own family well, with children who respect and obey him." (I Timothy 3:4 NLT) In my heart, I knew that this qualification was to be carefully considered and adhered to in all of life, especially for any high-ranking position, whether in church leadership or in business. The conclusion is definite and clear: The family must come first. Reconciling the conflicts between family and business is a KEY to release!

Producing a successful family in today's environment is the toughest job in the world. If the family is crowded out by your work hours and efforts, there is a bitter price to pay. If your spouse feels as though he or she is always playing second fiddle, there is no joy in family life.

A peek into the family life of an individual reveals a lot about the leadership of the parents and the attitudes of all family members. Through this window in a healthy, God-centered family you would observe mutual respect, enthusiastic obedience, and seriousness. The children are fun-loving but studious, and enjoy reading and listening to good music. The mutual love for each family member is evident in words and in deeds.

Recently I heard Dr. Henry Blackaby tell the story of consulting with a group seeking a new pastor for their church. He said, "Most folks look at educational background, speaking ability, and attractive appearance. Man looks on the outward appearance, but God looks on the heart! You must look into the heart of a man who would be your pastor."

The next question was a natural follow-up to this advice. "How do we look into his heart?" Dr. Blackaby's answer: "Go to his family— there you will discover his heart."

> *"The only rock I know that stays steady,*
> *the only institution I know that works is the family."*
> —Lee Iacocca

In order to build a strong, successful family, the relationship between husband and wife is crucial. There are so many situations related to our work that threaten this relationship in today's world. The traditional arrangement has been that the husband works outside the home and the wife stays at home with the children. Most often today both spouses are working outside the home.

Reconciling and more importantly preventing work-related conflict between you and your spouse is definitely a KEY. Higher level jobs generate more pressure to perform. Usually more travel and longer hours are required. This means spending less time with family. Putting family first is an exercise in planning and constant awareness of your priorities. Preventing work-related conflict between you and your spouse is the prime element in the KEY of Reconciliation.

When both spouses are working in professions that take them away from home, the wife may become the primary breadwinner. Her husband actually alters his work schedule to help with the children and upkeep of the home. Husband and wife may work together in the same company or in a business they own together. It may even be a home-based business. Whatever works best for the benefit of your entire family is an individual family decision. But do keep in mind that someone must be available to "keep the home fires burning."

One of the most attractive types of work today is telecommuting, which enables someone to work from home. Usually productivity increases, commuting expenses are eliminated, and the employee spends less on business attire. Years ago in our telemarketing department, there was a young woman who was a productive, industrious worker. All her associates appreciated her. When she was pregnant with her first child, she told us she would resign and stay at home with her new baby. The manager of that department asked if she would be willing to continue working if we supplied the tools she needed to work from her home. She agreed to try this arrangement. Much to our surprise, she actually increased her production while only working three days per week. She could do her work at her convenience and did not have to dress for the office or drive to work. The computer network automatically took care of placing her orders and tracking her work habits. She became her own boss in business for herself, and she thrived. We discovered this concept because of a mother's desire to stay at home with her baby. Working from home is now a common practice in business, and I believe it's a good practice for either gender.

There are many questions young couples face today that would not have been such a consideration in earlier years. They ask, "Should we have children? Will we be able to support additional family members on one income? Who will care for the children if both of us work outside the home?" A couple should discuss and mutually decide their priorities before marriage. If they rank income and possessions first, those priorities will always be at the expense of children. Children are a gift from the Lord, and many couples sacrifice this marvelous gift because of their chosen priorities.

A two-profession family with children must deal with the responsibility of rearing the children. Parents should ensure a Godly heritage that leads to salvation. Who is trustworthy with such a job? Could the grandparents participate in this responsibility? Is there affordable, quality childcare available? Would the children be exposed to values based on beliefs that are important to both parents?

A friend of ours, a radiologist, who continued her practice after her children were born, told us of her own experience. One day her young daughter commented, "Mommy, my nanny is more like my mommy than you are." This was a wake-up call for her. She immediately quit her job and stayed at home with her children full-time. However, I must add that not everyone is free to make this choice.

It has been my observation that many children today are left to their own supervision most of the time. They are free to watch television, play video games, and talk or text on their cell phones without adult supervision. Computer use is unlimited, and children have access to information that is inconsistent with a Biblical value system. Parents must be responsible to set guidelines and deadlines for their children. Children need to know that their activities are being observed. Children are a gift to the parents, and parents alone are responsible for their upbringing. Family must hold the top priority in your career decisions.

The husband-wife relationship is foundational to the building of a safe, secure, contented home. The successful family begins in the hearts of the mother and father. Harmony is an absolute necessity. Early in your relationship, agree on values to be lived and taught. Decide early on guidelines for discipline. My wife's book, *Bending the Twig*, is a must read on this subject. If it is too late to be early, rework your plan with your spouse and arrive at better resolutions that benefit everyone involved. Be prepared to discuss and resolve conflicts as they come to light. Be sensitive and do not sweep under the rug any work-related issues that create conflicts in your marriage or parental relationship. Leadership in reconciliation of any conflict is a must.

Ephesians 5 spells out priorities for the Christian family. The first requirement is that both spouses be filled with the Spirit (v. 5). When conflict occurs in your marriage, look first toward your individual walk with the Lord. When He is in control, there will be no long-lasting conflict because His Spirit does not conflict with Himself. Disagreements will happen perhaps, but an ongoing conflict should not! Mutual submission is the basis of teamwork in the home, "submitting to one another in the fear of God." (v. 21)

In all the organizations God has ordained, there is always a head, a CEO, someone who is responsible for the final decision. This does not infer inferiority on the part of the wife, but it is simply God's design, His way of "doing everything decently and in order." Ephesians 5:22-24 explains, "Wives, submit to your own husbands, as to the Lord. For the husband is the head of the wife, as also Christ is head of the church; and He is the Savior of the body. Therefore, just as the church is subject to Christ, so let the wives be to their own husbands in everything." No one can serve two masters, and someone must have the final word in order to avoid confusion in the home. Following God's pattern eliminates an unclear picture of roles for your children. Someone must be the leader and accept that final responsibility. As President Harry Truman said, "The buck stops here."

Scripture also gives clear instruction to husbands: "Husbands, love your wives, just as Christ also loved the church and gave Himself for her . . . . So husbands ought to love their own wives as their own bodies; he who loves his wife loves himself . . . . Nevertheless let each one of you in particular so love his own wife as himself, and let the wife see that she respects her husband." (Ephesians 5:25, 28, 33) Any wife convinced of her husband's depth and sincerity of true love undoubtedly will have little struggle with submitting to his direction.

A home built on the strength of a husband's love and a wife's respect is a solid foundation a Christian can count on. Throughout the Scriptures, we learn that our first priority in all of life is our relationship with the Lord. Our second priority is our relationship with our spouse. Children and the home are third. Work and ministry take the fourth position. It is always a struggle to set and hold to the Lord's guidelines. Under the demands of a high-pressure job, the battle of keeping order in our priorities becomes more intense. Adhering to the order of priority with a healthy, contented attitude is the foundation of the successful family.

> *"A man should never neglect his family for business."*
> —*Walt Disney*

Our church used to hold an annual church-wide wedding. All the couples that wanted to participate dressed up and marched down the aisle in the candlelit auditorium. During our 18th year of marriage, the pastor asked three people to give a testimony about their marriage, and I was one of those chosen. I was fearful to stand in front of that large crowd, yet I viewed it as a wonderful opportunity. It seemed to me that sharing in a humorous way would have the greatest impact, so my first comment was meant to be humorous. I began, "Our marriage was the climax of a torrid love affair. I was in love with myself, and I decided to let someone else in on it!" The audience roared with laughter. Sadly, this funny statement was the truth, and I knew it better than anyone, except Bernadine. I sensed that many marriages start on this basis, and I hoped that it would remain a thought-provoking statement for each couple. Somewhere along the line, I discovered that He is God—and I am not!

There are many situations that arise on the job that aggravate family relations, especially your relationship with your spouse. Working hours, travel away from home, and sexual temptation are the big three. There are other threatening problems, but time, travel, and relationships with associates of the opposite gender top the list of problem areas. These three big issues require thoughtful management. Any of these can blossom into an all-out shooting war between spouses unless anticipated and managed. We must practice "prevent defense" to avoid major conflicts at home.

Most jobs require a certain number of work hours each week. In order to be diligent, we should show up early, ready to work, and not rush out the door at the end of the day. However, it's easy to overdo this. Lengthy work hours can lead to the loss of family time. As you move up to higher positions, there will be even more pressure to get everything done even though you are no longer on the clock. Being diligent at work does not have to compete with dedication to your spouse and family.

Effective time management and avoiding time-wasters are great helps. Too much fellowship on the job can push necessary work to the end of the day. We must learn to be more effective and highly productive while working a full eight-hour day.

Communication with your spouse is critical; they should always be informed about your activities and requirements for each day. Your spouse needs to know what to expect. When your job requires entertainment or social events in the evening, make sure this is not a surprise for your mate.

Providing a copy of my updated calendar to my wife proved helpful as I moved up in the company. There were dinner meetings with customers, community and political events that were important to the business, and emergencies that required late hours. I made an effort to see that she was never surprised. In addition, I took her with me when it was appropriate. She frequently attended national sales meetings and recognition events. As she grew to understand more about my work, she appreciated my good job and our hard-working associates.

When we moved to Atlanta, my new job required heavy travel, meaning I was away from home more than 50 percent of the time. My wife did an excellent job of taking care of our home and children in my absence. Each family is unique, and personalities, talents, abilities, strengths, weaknesses, and preferences will have to be considered as you contemplate your job requirements.

If a particular job promotion, relocation, or other change would put family members in an awkward, uncomfortable role for which they are not especially suited, the resolution of the problem must be anticipated before any decision is made. In every case, no commitment to change jobs, especially those involving relocation, should be made without the full support of your spouse. There are definitely times when a promotion that requires relocation should be declined. Timing and family situations are a big factor. Both spouses must fully support the move with a whole heart.

There was a promising young man who worked in our Dallas office. We had our eyes on him for big things in the future. When we approached him about relocating to Atlanta, he was hesitant. His wife's parents were located near his work and she did not want to move.

Finally, he convinced her that he should take this promotion, and they moved. She was miserable, downcast, and constantly complained. A short time later he agreed to a demotion. They returned to Texas; his career was stymied. Halfhearted agreement will never work. Sadly, a few years later they were divorced.

When away from home, the primary defense against conflict is good communication. Cell phones and email are invaluable. Touch base at home each day. Be prepared to weigh in on important decisions. If necessary, travel late and hard to be home for big events. Other outside activities may need to be sacrificed in order to have more time at home. During our children's formative years, I gave up golf except for corporate events. No matter what your hobbies, your investment of time with your spouse and children will prove more valuable than activities in which they cannot participate.

Time invested in family is the greatest gift you can give them. Spend time with the children. When they are young, get on the floor and play with them. After working all day and especially with added travel, there is the temptation to just "chill out" with television or reading. With such an attitude, the family does not benefit whether you are at home or away. My wife once said in jest that if I died, she would just spread a *Wall Street Journal* over my recliner and everyone would think I was still there.

My wife encouraged me to spend special time with our only son, and we joined the Indian Guides, a father-son organization sponsored by the YMCA. For several years, we owned a lake house where we often enjoyed family outings. We valued our time away from the distractions involved on the home front, but we were also cautious to make sure church attendance was a priority, even when we were away. We hoped that holding to this priority would illustrate to our children that recreation, sports, and leisure never took precedence over our relationship with the Lord. Certainly, church activities are vitally important; your participation clearly demonstrates your priorities to your children.

Time devoted to your family speaks much louder than words or gifts. A few years ago, our son wrote a letter that has been a lasting encouragement to me in my retirement. He wrote, "Dad you were the consummate workaholic, but you always showed up for everything that was important to me."

A real and present danger for those who travel often is detachment or abdication of responsibility. One of my friends had a job that required full-time travel. Eventually he came to enjoy time away more than his time at home. He willingly abdicated his responsibilities as a father. The results were disappointing and sad for everyone. Near the end of his life, he greatly regretted the loss.

In my career we relocated four times. My wife is an only child and extremely close to her family, but she was always supportive. I never accepted a promotion without discussing it with her. She was always committed to my career and was quick to make adjustments. She was a true partner in my work, and she always kept the home fires burning. Spending time together discussing your work allows your spouse to better understand what you do, and they will be more supportive if they know what is going on at work. I now wish I had spent even more time helping my wife feel that she was an important aspect of my business success.

The third, most devastating conflict comes about as a result of our association with co-workers of the opposite gender. In today's workplace, such associations are a fact of life and cannot be avoided. When I started my career, there were virtually no females in my business except in office work. Just a few years later, our sales force was 20-percent female. Women came on board as customer service representatives, and several held management positions. The work situation had totally changed. Male and female associates spend more time with one another than with spouses. This can create an unhealthy tension. How do we play "prevent defense" when these conditions exist as a necessary part of the job?

First and foremost, we must hang out the "not available" sign. This means no flirtation, no matter how innocent. It means speaking frequently of your spouse on the job. It means making your commitment to your spouse obvious in casual conversation. Readily available family pictures on display in your office and in your wallet send a message. Your eyes, your comments, your jokes, and your appropriate responses to the more attractive young associates will go a long way in maintaining your spouse's confidence.

> *"Never be alone with a woman who is not your wife."*
> —Billy Graham

In my experience, I found that by giving my wife assurance and confirmation of my commitment, this enabled her to become all that the Lord has said she is to be. Genesis 2:18 uses the word *helpmeet* which means suitable, adapted, completing. Your wife will feel significant in her role as she places her trust in you because she knows that she is your first priority.

Always establish ground rules early in your business relationships with those of the opposite gender. When I met with the young woman who was promoted to vice president of human resources, I shared a lot of information about my family with her. Since she would be reporting to me, I also mentioned that we might have lunch together, but we would never be alone. Vera smiled; she was in total agreement.

When traveling to the same location, I never sat with a female associate on the airplane. Being aware that there were aggressive, ambitious young women who would flirt and get too close motivated me to keep my guard up, just as everyone should!

If possible, make opportunity for your spouse to meet and get to know those of the opposite gender whom you work with closely. Involve your spouse as much as possible in direct-reporting relationships. Actually, my wife recommended the vice president of human resources referred to earlier. She knew her, admired her abilities, and trusted my interaction with her.

In order to prevent uncertainty on the part of your spouse, selection and training of a personal assistant is critical. When I became national sales manager, I was entitled to administrative support. I was blessed to inherit the retired owner's assistant. Betty became a family friend. My wife and the entire family loved her. When Betty retired, I was faced with the task of finding a new assistant. Perhaps my experience will help you avoid the land mines.

It is not wise to hire anyone as an assistant until your spouse interviews and approves. The assistant should never compete with your spouse in any way. An assistant will have full-time access to your schedule and activities. Your communication, with the cooperation of the assistant, to keep your spouse abreast of your schedule will provide the necessary assurance. Your directions must be clear; your spouse has first priority. Your assistant's respectful response to your spouse will affirm his or her standing.

Allowing your spouse high-priority access to you is vital. If necessary, install a direct line so that your spouse can always get to you without going through the "gatekeeper." But, the gatekeeper can be effective when demonstrating a pleasant, healthy attitude toward your spouse, which you should always encourage. Having a cell phone with text messaging could be a helpful tool in communicating with your spouse. The whole idea—there is an unwritten "no compete agreement!"—that is almost as evident as a written contract.

It was my policy to keep the door of my office open for meetings with female associates. A mutual agreement with your assistant of no private meetings—all doors open removes potential suspicion of co-workers and avoids uncomfortable or awkward situations. Sexual harassment laws are a great benefit to businesses of all types. Modern society and relaxed attitudes regarding fraternization has caused office relationships to become a major problem. This law enables companies to make policies based on the law rather than moralizing. Of course, it should be evident that the law only reinforces the moral convictions of the leader.

Speaking as a man with years of experience, I have observed that a leader who is sexually immoral becomes weaker in his role as a leader. A leader's heart must be focused on the security of his family as he develops his career. This focus cannot be obtained and maintained if he is open to being in wrong relationships. For the moral man, inappropriate relationships usually begin with a seemingly innocent emotional attraction. A man must guard his heart—and his zipper!

Strength for "prevent defense" is found in the intimate relationship between a husband and wife. "Because there is so much sexual immorality, each man should have his own wife, and each woman should have her own husband. The husband should not deprive his wife of sexual intimacy, which is her right as a married woman, nor should the wife deprive her husband. The wife gives authority over her body to her husband, and the husband also gives authority over his body to his wife. So do not deprive each other of sexual relations. The only exception to this rule would be the agreement of both husband and wife to refrain from sexual intimacy for a limited time, so they can give themselves more completely to prayer. Afterward they should come together again so that Satan won't be able to tempt them because of their lack of self-control." (I Corinthians 7:2-5 NLT)

Discover the ways that your spouse is a complement to you. Even if your spouse does not "meet your needs," you are accountable to the Lord to keep your behavior above reproach. Besides keeping a sound relationship with your spouse and soundness in your relationship with the Lord, remaining pure is even more job security.

When couples discuss their difficulties, financial struggles head the list. As in all matters, openness between husband and wife is vital! There should be no secret bank accounts and no big expenditures without the spouse's knowledge. There seems to be a widespread distrust between husbands and wives. Husbands often have secret accounts. Some wives have little sales resistance and purchase without consideration of their financial situation or their husband's desires. Such practices by either spouse are a recipe for disaster.

After only a few days of marriage, Bernadine caught my financial attention. She balanced the bank statement. She discovered $100 (a lot of dough to this young man) of which I had no knowledge. Women are *usually* more detail-minded. Men, if you miss this aspect of sharing and consulting with your wife, you will miss a great blessing. Many men think of their wives as emotional and not financially astute. Don't limit your thinking about your wife with generalities. Discover her individual strengths and weaknesses.

Over the years, I discovered that Bernadine's financial advice was most often sound. Once we were touring an investment property facility in Savannah that had tax advantages because of its historical preservation status. Apparently my wife was observing the salesperson as closely as she was studying the property. When driving back to Atlanta she said, "Hopefully you wouldn't consider investing with that fellow no matter how good it seems. He told several lies in the short time that we were together." Based on her assessment, I declined the offer. I had not noticed the lies. A friend did invest in that property and lost every penny, plus penalties. Bernadine's observations of inconsistencies saved us a big financial failure.

My wife didn't like the idea of any tax-avoidance schemes. She believed that I was considering such an investment because of a bad attitude regarding taxes. Her tongue-in-cheek comment was, "I know how you can avoid this problem. Just don't make much money." She reminded me that Jesus said, "Render unto Caesar the things that are Caesar's and unto God the things that are God's." She shared some other thoughts, such as the benefits that the government provided for us—freeways, airports, military protection and much more. One time she even suggested that I send in a little extra money with our tax return to compensate for my bad attitude.

The "hook was set" and in spite of her advice, I "invested" in a tax shelter. Several years later, the IRS filed suit in federal court against the participants in this tax shelter. We lost the case. We paid four times the tax savings in penalties and interest. From that point, I never made another investment without listening to my wife's opinion. There was never another thought of investing in a "tax shelter." I had learned an expensive lesson; it had been a big mistake driven by greed. That loss confirmed that "tax shelters" were often temporary and resulted in losses down the road. In other words, there's always a payday someday!

Listen to your spouse's judgment. View your spouse as an advisor and mentor. Together, you make a complete unit. We should never be independent of our spouse, although they may not have our expertise and sophisticated knowledge of the situation. This is particularly true of a husband regarding his wife. It seems the Lord has given women a sixth sense. Often, they cannot explain in a practical way how they reach their conclusion. Always consider her thoughts. There will never be anyone else in your life that has the capacity to love you, support you, and provide advice with only your best interest at heart. Truly, in marriage, we are a team. Consider both team members' thoughts when making decisions. Don't miss out on this blessing!

Now that I've retired, the most enjoyable time of each day is when we get up in the morning. With a cup of coffee in hand, we read the Scriptures and consult the Lord on the issues we are facing. Unfortunately, I missed this for years because of my need to get to work early. If I could do it over, I'd get up earlier! You must not miss this time of togetherness—praying, studying, and talking. Men should take the lead as head of the family. There is an old cliché: "The family that prays together stays together." There can be no doubt that this discipline when practiced with a full and open heart will be blessed by the Lord. He answers prayer!

"No matter what you've done for yourself or for humanity, if you can't look back on having given love and attention to your own family, what have you really accomplished?"
—*Elbert Hubbard*

During my years as CEO, the press often interviewed me. One of their favorite questions was, "What has been your greatest success?" Of course, they were fishing for a new product, an acquisition, or some dramatic, world-changing discovery. My answer was always the same: "My greatest success is my family!"

Let there be no misunderstanding that the release of your CEO within depends on your commitment to family and home life. Business success is insignificant and miserable when the family fails.

"As the family goes, so goes the nation and so goes the whole world in which we live."
—*Pope John Paul II*

Chapter Nine

The Key of Revitalization

Finding purpose in all of life

Suddenly, I was a CEO! Throughout my career, I had often dreamed of making our company different, and now I was in the position to initiate that change. As CEO, I could drive us toward a vision that I had only imagined. A great feeling of release engulfed me as I began the journey.

My hope of bringing about change stemmed from my childhood, learned through the belief system that upheld our little town. For the most part, a "good name" (Proverbs 22:1) was worth more than gold in that community of yesteryear.

As I faced this marvelous leadership opportunity and the challenge of building a vision for our company, questions were popping into my thoughts. Could this "good name" principle be reproduced in a large business? Just how important is reputation for a business? Does it relate to growth and profits in any way?

The value the community placed on a good name became reality in my first real job—a paper route. In my everyday duties as a paperboy, I realized others' expectations and came to deeply value the preferences of my customers. They loved the special care I gave, like putting the paper behind the screen door. They appreciated the fact that I delivered the paper no matter what the weather—snow, rain, cold winter days, or hot summer days. Some customers even gave me lavish tips for my good service. Without realizing what was happening, valuing customers became part of my belief system. Customers' good will and satisfaction with the product was of primary importance and would ultimately contribute strongly to growth.

When our company acquired 3M's copier/fax business on a worldwide basis, we combined it with our copier operations along with a few folks from the parent company. When I met with the management team, I was somewhat surprised at the diversity. The team represented three rather different business cultures, a fascinating challenge. In addition, we had businesses in Europe and Latin America. There was great strength in the diversity of thought that emanated from this new team.

A few days later we had our first strategic planning meeting. Our primary objective was to determine the purpose of our company. In years past, when questioning others about purpose in business, most often the answer was profits. This simple bottom-line answer seemed narrow and potentially dangerous to me. I entered that first meeting with determination to dig for deeper reason and motive for our newly formed joint venture. My heart was set on finding a purpose that would support my childhood belief system.

After much discussion about our strengths and weaknesses, our team honed in on customer satisfaction as our purpose. But we took it a step further. We purposed that we would be the *best* in customer satisfaction. As a new CEO with a dream of change, I was deeply impressed with such a diverse group of people having total harmony around this idea.

Shortly after my retirement, Lanier won the J.D. Power Award for being best in customer satisfaction. I felt a great deal of personal satisfaction; our purpose had continued on to fulfillment and was now independently documented and recognized. What were the elements in this achievement? What were the actions taken to make this dream a reality?

There is no greater motivation in any life or any business than to have a clearly defined purpose. There is an immense release of passion, energy, and excitement in an individual's life when purpose is defined and achieved. This same truth applies to any organization!

In order to create a purpose in an organization, it must be preceded by vision. From the leader's vision, the purpose can be determined. When there is no vision, the people just wander around aimlessly. (Proverbs 29:18) Vision flows from the leader. Vision illuminates and enables your followers to visualize where the organization is headed.

I recently visited with the chief of police of Woodstock. He asked a significant question, "When you cast a vision do you just announce it to your people, or do you allow them to participate so that you have buy-in immediately?" What a great question! It leads right in to a particularly important step in the process of creating a clearly defined purpose for an organization. Going before the leaders of any organization and asking them to vote on any new direction of their choice indicates weak leadership. Achieving alignment is the specific responsibility of the leader. The leader presents ideas and leadership stories, using a collaborative style to gain support for new ideas. Even in the face of opposition, an effective leader will gain support through persuasion.

The concept of building our company on this "good name" principle was foremost in my thoughts as I prepared for the strategic planning meeting. "A good name is to be chosen rather than great riches, loving favor rather than silver and gold." (Proverbs 22:1)

I was anticipating our company placing the highest value on a good name—a rock-solid reputation with all constituents, beginning with our customers. Much attention is automatically focused on profits, but everyone knows that customers are the only source of revenues. Only from revenue is there a potential for hiring employees (each one of us) and making a profit (keeping shareholders happy).

Since this was my first meeting with the management team since I became CEO and our organization was newly formed, I decided to facilitate the meeting personally rather than bringing in a professional facilitator. I felt it was necessary that I put my identity on the organization and establish myself as the leader.

Not long into the discussion of our company's strengths and weaknesses, we easily saw the potential of our becoming a powerful organization. By capitalizing on those many strengths and overcoming the weaknesses of the three original organizations, we could become a formidable competitor. With just a few gentle nudges on my part, the idea of focusing on customer satisfaction came to the forefront. There was strong enthusiasm for the idea and it gained momentum, progressing to the goal of being the best in customer satisfaction. By the end of the meeting, this basic purpose was fleshed out with a long to-do list.

Measurements were at the core of this discussion. We needed a means of knowing that we were accomplishing our goal. The primary measurement would be customer loyalty. If the customer continued to purchase our products presently and in the future we had the ultimate proof of customer satisfaction. Using loyalty as the primary measurement eliminated the "opinion poll" concept commonly used to measure customer satisfaction.

Our leadership team invested a great deal of time in planning. As Luke 14:28 reminds us, planning is priceless. "Which of you, intending to build a tower, does not sit down first and count the cost, whether he has enough to finish it?" If you craft a vision and purpose that sail directly into gale force winds, you are predetermining defeat. Wise strategic planning must include the study of major competitors. Jesus gave instructions regarding competition. "What king, going to make war against another king, does not sit down first and consider whether he is able with ten thousand to meet him who comes against him with twenty thousand?" (Luke 14:31)

There were surprises when we began measuring customer loyalty for our own company and for our competitors. The first surprise was not a pleasant one. Our customer loyalty was only 47 percent based on a study conducted by an independent consulting firm. We did receive some good news. All our competitors were in the same boat—or even worse. Our largest and most feared competitor had the largest market share and the lowest customer loyalty. We welcomed that surprise as a major opportunity.

The market study revealed a constant churning of the copiers in use in the marketplace. It seemed that everyone disliked their presently owned copier regardless of the brand.

A major customer in San Francisco told me that he hated all copiers. "They all break down constantly—the whole design is a recipe for mechanical failure. We just buy the one with the best service." That customer's confirmation gave credence to our new purpose. The more we learned about the market, the more momentum was generated for our new direction.

Perhaps one of the most memorable strategic statements regarding competition came from a highly respected baseball manager:

> *"Hit it where they ain't."*
> —*Casey Stengel*

Any ad agency worth their salt understands this axiom of success. As we planned our advertising for the year, we presented our new strategy to our advertising agency. They came back to us with an unconventional proposal that featured a startling promise. It was to be called the Lanier Performance Promise and would be the first of its kind for our industry. The promise was supported entirely by our desire to be the best in customer satisfaction, and it guaranteed uptime, offered replacement of any copier that was unsatisfactory at the customer's direction, as well as several other distinctive guarantees that made us stand out in our desire to please the customer. It was a bold statement and seemed like a stretch at this point in our development. After carefully considering the terms of our promise and its cost, we decided to go with it. This provided a strong competitive advantage for us. Just a few years later a similar promise was offered by every major copier supplier, clearly documenting the effectiveness of the idea. Not only did our promise make a statement to our customers and prospects, it made a colossal statement to our associates regarding our seriousness about our purpose.

As we began to implement the focus on customer satisfaction throughout the company, we began to see training and systems needs that were not evident previously. A great strength of our company had always been our customer service representatives. They were in constant contact and were the face of our company to the customer. We designed a customer relations program in order to improve relationship skills, and this required a major investment in their training.

Through our customer research we discovered that response time and completing repairs in one visit were of major importance to the customer. We invested in systems that tracked all major elements, such as response time, down time, and callbacks. Copy quality was important to the customer. At increased expense, we replaced parts as necessary to bring copy quality up to standards each time we serviced a copier.

Those are just a few of many important investments made in order to improve customer satisfaction. When a new direction is announced, every employee watches to see if it's just the flavor of the day or if it is a real, in-depth, permanent process change. If you are not willing to invest in the program, no one will believe it's truly important. They are right in reaching that conclusion.

We looked for a memorable slogan for our national sales meeting. We wanted it to be a call to arms that would rally our troops across the nation around our new purpose. Lance Herrin, vice president of U.S. operations, came to my office with a big smile on his face. The promotions agency we were working with came up with the perfect answer: "Customer Vision." It was defined as seeing everything through the eyes of the customer with an objective of meeting or exceeding their expectations. I knew immediately that it was perfect.

The National Sales Meeting was only the beginning of the universal use of this slogan. Customer Vision was featured in all advertising and promotions and was the headline in all recognition programs. All employees wore a Customer Vision pin. A special 18-carat-gold version was created and awarded to those who did heroic acts for the customer. The program took on a life of its own as it was institutionalized. It was challenging, exciting, and fun for everyone, especially the customers! We were creating a totally new culture throughout the company, a culture that focused on the customer and provided substance to our quest for a "good name."

In our sales organization, there was a tendency to occasionally overstate or promise things we couldn't deliver. The emphasis on customer satisfaction immediately removed that temptation. Any overstatements were revealed and exposed in short order. The new order was under-promise and over-deliver!

As we began to make progress, people asked, "What is the difference in the way you run the company and in the way your predecessor did it?" My answer: "He started his career as a salesman working for a dealer. He primarily ran the company for the benefit of sales reps and/or dealers. My intent is to run the company for the benefit of the customers." Perhaps this was a subtle difference to some folks, but it was most important in getting all associates coupled to the purpose of our business and working in alignment for the common good of our customers.

Recognition is important in any organization. Employee surveys indicate that recognition ranks extremely high on employee satisfaction, right up there with other benefits such as compensation. It follows that in any organization recognition should be tied to the purpose, especially during the transformation process. The speed of implementation and productivity increases rapidly with the excitement and motivation of recognition.

Fran Tarkington tells a story that clearly illustrates this fact. While Tarkington was playing for the Minnesota Vikings, Bud Grant called a "gadget play." In order for this play to work, the quarterback had to successfully make a key block. Usually quarterbacks are protected and not asked to do anything that is personally risky. The quarterback's unexpected involvement was a major element in the design of the play.

Tarkington threw the key block and they executed the play perfectly, resulting in winning the game. The following week as the team reviewed the game films, the coach commented about several plays but said nothing about the key block that made the gadget play effective. Privately, Tarkington asked the coach about his neglect. The coach responded, "Fran, you're a professional. You always carry out your assignments. I didn't think it was necessary to mention it." Tarkington replied, "It wasn't necessary—unless you should ever want me to do it again!"

To my delight, more and more often I heard stories of acts of service above and beyond the call of duty that our people were performing for our customers. I often traveled to the location and made a personal presentation of the gold Customer Vision pin to the employee who had performed the heroic deed. Special recognition highlighting desired behavior is an integral part of transformation.

The three "C"s of leadership (Communicate, Communicate, Communicate) never have more importance than when an organization faces a time of transformation and revitalization. Each quarter we highlighted a Customer Vision hero story in our video that reported quarterly events.

In a short time our customer loyalty improved to 90 percent, moving into the area experts call the "sweet spot." Dataquest, a market research firm, conducted a customer satisfaction survey by brand name. Toshiba was ninth on the list and Lanier was first. Since Toshiba made most of our products, the survey plainly indicated that there is more to customer satisfaction than just the product. The product has to be exceptional, but there are many other ingredients. We were beginning to fully understand and categorize all the nuts and bolts of customer satisfaction and loyalty.

Our company often had motivational speakers at our national sales meetings. They inspired listeners to commitment, energy, and increased productivity. Many were from the field of athletics, including Jimmy Valvano, Roger Staubach, John Wooden, and Joe Theisman. Purpose in their vocational field is simple. The purpose is to win! It is clear, it is simple, and it is direct; just go out there and win. That is one reason they are so effective in communication. There is no confusion of their ultimate purpose. Why can't we make it that uncomplicated in business?

The renowned coach Vince Lombardi always told his team there are only three important things in your life. Focus on these things and these things only: God, family, and the Green Bay Packers! His message was always punctuated by this oft-repeated phrase: "Winning isn't everything—it's the only thing!"

Great leaders develop short memorable statements that keep on point and simplify their message. It would be difficult to misunderstand them. Ronald Reagan was often asked his strategy for winning the Cold War. His answer was simple: "We win—they lose!"

When Steve Jobs founded Apple, he described their computers as a bicycle of the mind. This was a great word picture for simplifying his thoughts for the future of the information age. Computers would be low-cost, simple, natural, and easy for anyone to use, just like a bicycle. Determining a purpose is not easy for many businesses. It requires much thought, reflection, and creativity. The purpose must be simply expressed.

> *"Don't underestimate the power of a vision. McDonald's founder, Ray Kroc, pictured his empire long before it existed, and he saw how to get there. He invented the company motto — 'Quality, service, cleanliness, and value' — and kept repeating it to employees for the rest of his life."*
> —Kenneth Labich

No matter the size of your organization, your purpose must not reflect the egocentric approach of wealth for a few. Purpose statements including elements like putting the competitors out of business or making shareholders rich are extremely selfish and even dangerous. Customer focus must be included, which means you must determine who the customer is. Unfortunately, this is not clear for many organizations, such as schools, churches, and government operations. A fuzzy definition of the customer will always result in a fuzzy and confusing purpose.

I once worked on a Chamber of Commerce committee to elect school board members for a major city school system that was failing miserably. During the process I asked the key leaders, "Who do you see as the customers for the schools? Who are you aiming to satisfy?" The answer they gave was "society." I had thought the answer might be the parents who are legally responsible for the children. How about the businesses and organizations that might hire the students when they graduated? How about the colleges and universities where they might attend? What about the students themselves? Surely there could be a clearly defined customer for education. Usually the customer is the one who pays for the product.

A wonderful example of a company with a clearly defined purpose is Walmart. "Always low prices" has been the driving force of this company since Sam Walton founded it. Customers love it, employees can easily see the good work they are doing, and the shareholders have been rewarded as well. Other companies such as Service Master and Wells Real Estate Funds have thought-provoking vision statements that spotlight glorifying God.

The enthusiasm and productivity that come to an organization motivated by purpose is a wonderful thing to behold. The retired chairman of Porsche, the German automobile manufacturer, told a story that illustrates this fact. Porsche entered the Le Mans race regularly. The race is named for the city of Le Mans, France, and uses some public roads for a circuit that is just over eight miles long. The objective is to cover as much distance as possible in the 24-hour period.

Porsche had entered two cars in the race, and at about 3:00 a.m. one of the cars came into the pit for repairs. Quick diagnosis determined that a clutch bearing had failed. The good news—the bearing cost only $3.72. The bad news—by the book it was more than a three-hour repair job. The mid-engine car had to have the transmission separated from the engine in order to make this repair.

The pit area was simply a tent. It was cold and rainy. There was no food. The technicians attacked that car. Their gloves were smoking, but they were on a mission. They replaced the bearing in 38 minutes and Porsche won the race.

Who were these guys? This is the big surprise. They were volunteers; they received no pay for this job. They were regular shop-floor employees who consistently argued for better working conditions and more pay. Under these dire conditions, with a clear purpose, they were entirely transformed. In auto racing, as in athletics, the purpose is clear. When we duplicate this in any organization, productivity will soar!

> *"The companies that survive the longest are the ones that work out what they can uniquely give to the world—not just growth or money, but their excellence, their respect for others, their ability to make people happy. Some call those things a soul."*
> —*Charles Handy*

Every individual should have an individual life purpose in mind and heart. You may never be in the position to help shape the purpose of an organization, but you can shape your personal purpose. If you have not thoughtfully determined your purpose, consider this same process. The same concepts are applicable for the individual as for organizational purpose statements.

Jesus gives the Biblical model of this principle of purpose when he launched the New Testament church at the time of His ascension. "Go therefore and make disciples of all nations, baptizing them in the name of the Father and of the Son and of the Holy Spirit, teaching them to observe all that I have commanded you. And behold, I am with you always, to the end of the age." (Matthew 28:19-20 ESV)

Jesus was leaving His disciples and He gave them a mission statement. This statement provided purpose for all He had called them to do. This purpose was so powerful that His disciples literally gave their lives to launch the church in the entire Mediterranean region. They left home, risked life and limb, were imprisoned, beaten, and shipwrecked. They were willing to put everything on the line so that His purpose could be fulfilled. The church was established and has continued to grow for over 2,000 years.

Jesus' directive focused on the major activities of the church. It was simple and easy to remember. The major purpose was to lead people to Christ and teach them to obey all the teachings of Jesus. The most comforting thing He said was His promise to be with us always. No doubt this was not completely understood at the time of His ascension, but at Pentecost the disciples witnessed firsthand the power of the Holy Spirit and His presence in Christians' lives. We easily overlook the great enabling power of the indwelling Spirit of God even today, and we find ourselves working in the strength of the flesh. We must always remember that Jesus said all power is His and He would be with us always.

The mission given to us by Jesus is the underlying purpose of every Christian life. Does your life purpose support the Christian mission? Your concepts of success, wealth, and God are all critical in determining your purpose. If you grow into a leadership position or if you are in a leadership role presently, you can influence the purpose of your organization. The concept of purpose is the KEY motivational force to transform or revitalize your personal walk with the Lord as well as any organization with which you are associated. Once you know your purpose, the work flows, the motivation rises and productivity is at an all time high. Focusing on your purpose will accelerate the release of your CEO within!

Chapter 10

Redefining Success

Determine your destination

Each year, we enjoy attending the Horatio Alger inaugural event in Washington. We are privileged to hear the stories of the young students receiving Horatio Alger scholarships. Their stories of hardship and difficulty remind me of the value of making foundational choices early in life.

Brandon, an engaging African-American young man with a big smile, received a scholarship in 2008. His life struggles were exposed as he described his absentee father whom he never knew, his drug-addicted mother, and the difficult community life where he grew up. Aside from the obviously discouraging circumstances, his peers told Brandon repeatedly that he would never get out of the neighborhood. The choices for young men there were limited: join a gang, sell dope, or pimp.

Brandon's older brothers made wrong choices; one was killed and the other imprisoned. On the other hand, Brandon is positive of his destination. He has adopted an entirely different framework for his future. He draws strength from his faith in Christ and participation in his church. Brandon's positive outlook has been determined partially by his desire to set a proper example for his younger sisters and to take care of them. Brandon's grandmother was easy to spot at the ceremony because of her big smile; Brandon was the first in his family to graduate from high school.

As Brandon and other young scholars shared their stories, I kept hearing the phrase "adversity builds character." Brandon's brothers had faced the exact same adversities he had, yet they took a different path. The phrase, though often used, is only partially correct. Adversity does not build character; an individual's response to adversity determines the outcome. The correct response builds character.

The destination of every life is the product of a series of decisions or choices made along the way. Some choices may not seem important at the time, but later you realize they have major impact on the results produced. Brandon has made a choice in life that will determine his future if he continues to hold fast to this early choice. It's particularly rewarding when this choice concerning destination is made early in life rather than later.

> *"Attitude is a deep-seated, chosen belief, either positive or negative, that sets in motion corresponding behavior, generally resulting in a self-fulfilling prophecy."*
> —*Michael Q. Pink*

Perhaps nothing affects your attitude and overall accomplishment in life as much as your belief about your own destination. That belief forms a framework that will shape all your decisions. For me, that framework comprised a definition of success that evolved as I moved through life.

The most popular view of success is getting all you can, displaying your wealth with houses, clothing, fine cars, and the like. Position and power are a big part of the mix. We see the results of many bad choices based on the unrelenting pursuit of this brand of success. Unfortunately, defining success for most of us is a gradual process. It is my conviction that we should adopt, as Brandon has, an enlightened definition early in life. I want to encourage you to speed the process and assure the release of the CEO within by determining your destination early in your career.

> *The tragedy of life is not that it ends so soon,*
> *but that we wait so long to begin it!*
> *Anonymous*

There were several experiences in my childhood that shaped my early concept of success. My family did not have much monetarily, sometimes only the bare essentials. There were many discussions regarding money—or the lack thereof. These discussions had a profound impact on my thinking. Put simply, I did not want to be poor.

In an infrequent but treasured conversation, I discussed my educational aspirations with my dad. I was considering teaching and coaching. His prompt response was, "You will never make much money, and teaching requires that you give your life to the children." He shared his observations of my money-making endeavors. That settled it for me. I decided to pursue a career in technology since I had such a love of electronics. The unspoken desire never to be poor was the greatest influencing factor in the choice.

There were only two things in my thoughts that framed my definition of success as I began my career: a good job and a new car. My barber frequently reminded me of his definition of success: "All you need in life is a good car and a good woman." My definition was short and limited at that time, but it would change radically over the next few years.

"All you need for happiness is a good gun, a good horse, and a good wife."
—Daniel Boone

Things did change, and new standards came on the scene when the company transferred me to Baton Rouge, Louisiana. Quite different from my previous job, there was an expected daily productivity in repairing and servicing equipment. The number of customer calls completed each day was carefully monitored. The company offered me a pleasant and surprising opportunity to earn commissions on sales of service contracts and sales leads. I often wonder if it was obvious that I enjoyed the money, power, and freedom that job provided. My definition of success became even narrower—leaning more towards earning lots of money. Envy became a part of my thought process as I observed the salesmen and saw that they earned two or three times my income with seemingly much less effort.

Those early days' experiences shaped my future in other ways as well. Having graduated at the top of my class, I thought highly of myself. Pride led to two distinct patterns of failure. In repairing office machines, I often failed to finish the job, resulting in a callback. My technical knowledge was superb, but I was caught up in technical analysis and overlooked simple problems with simple solutions. Secondly, there was the issue of customer relations. In many cases I talked down to the customer. If I thought they were misusing the product, I quickly blamed them for the problem.

Bernadine's boss at the time added a humiliating and challenging comment that pricked my pride even more. When she told him that we were engaged to be married, he said, "You can do better than marrying a screwdriver mechanic."

One kind customer suggested that I read Dale Carnegie's book, *How to Win Friends and Influence People.* I wondered why he suggested it. When I read the book, its message came through clearly. Without humility we cannot learn, and I had lots to learn. I began to see my customers from a different perspective. Something especially important happened: Humility had touched my heart. Any successful career involves lifelong learning. Humility opens that door.

When the company offered me the opportunity to open an office in Gulfport, Mississippi, I eagerly accepted the challenge. Previously, two employees had been sent to this location and both had failed. This was a great chance to prove myself. Bernadine and I had spent our short honeymoon on that beautiful coast. We thought it would be nice to live there, and that casual dream became a reality.

The location was lovely, and the opportunity to sell as well as to service products was a challenging and exciting prospect. A combination sales and service job afforded the potential of earning much more money. My definition of success was still related to money, and now there was added the prestige of winning sales contests and seeing my name at the top. Competition and comparison would give me the chance to be a top producer.

We bought our first house in Gulfport, and our first two children were born there. Becoming a family man certainly added weight to my already inflated view of the need for money in order to be successful.

In only two years, I was transferred to Augusta, Georgia. This was my first management experience although there was only one employee to manage. My priority was selling products, and the customer service representative did repairs and maintenance with my occasional help and supervision. It was thrilling to win the first annual sales contest—a trip to Acapulco—and Bernadine was included. This was a "feather in my cap" and was added to my inflated view of success.

Shortly after that big win, I hit a slump. Sales were minimal. With the cold reality of earnings totally based on commission staring me in the face, I knew that something had to be done. Depression and a lack of enthusiasm became my nagging, unwanted companions. It is hard to sell anything without enthusiasm.

Considering our circumstances, we made a decision that seemed illogical at the time. We decided to give 10 percent of our income to the Lord's work. The decision to tithe was important, but it was not nearly as important as my acceptance of the fact that God owns it ALL!

My vocation began to take on a new meaning as I saw myself as an overseer of a portion of the Lord's work, managing some of His resources. I began the transformation from being a taker to becoming a giver. The principle of Luke 19:17—that those who are faithful in little things will be given responsibility for big things—became a serious part of my thought process. This had an immediate and permanent impact on my definition of success and determining my destination.

When the offer came to return to Baton Rouge as district manager, I was delighted. As we prepared for the move, I enjoyed thinking of the beginning of my career in that location. I knew Bernadine was happy to be living near her parents again. We were both elated. A district manager had the authority to make almost all decisions related to district operations. This position afforded a healthy income opportunity as well. Overall, I thought that this was the best position in the company and that I was best suited for management.

Fear was a nagging enemy as I recalled the stories of many salesmen who became managers, but failed. They were good salesman, but they didn't make good managers. There was much to be learned. Management is a totally different job, requiring new and different skills from those I had learned as a salesman.

It was good to be greeted by members of the old Baton Rouge team. It was comforting to see those folks I knew and had worked with previously. But even with all the pleasure of returning, this became the toughest period of my career up to that point. My new boss, who was to teach me how to be a manager, was present to greet me. He was bright and creative, but I soon discovered that his value system was vastly different from mine. It became apparent that he didn't enjoy being with me and I had the unpleasant feeling that he really wanted me to fail. He often said, "Nice guys finish last!" His message was that I wasn't tough or mean enough to succeed in this job.

In addition to dealing with a difficult authority situation, there was a serious problem with one of my direct reports that I spoke of in a previous chapter. Production numbers exposed the fact that I was failing as district manager. My emotions were following suit. Failure was miserable! To make things even worse, the sale of our house in Augusta fell through, and the financial and emotional pressure became intense. This was the only time in my entire career that I actually interviewed for another job.

One night my wife suggested we attend church to hear a guest speaker. Unexpectedly, I heard a message that changed the remainder of my career dramatically. It also drastically changed my definition of success. The thought provoking title for the talk was "Heaven on Earth." For me, it was better than the title! Personal lessons poured out through that message. Like a man stranded in the desert with all hope gone, I stumbled upon an oasis. The Water of the Word flowed over my thirsty soul as I listened to the confirming and affirming words. There was assurance: Christ dwelt in me in the power of the Holy Spirit and would never depart. There was revelation: Christ would transform my life, guiding and directing me into His plan for my life. It was evident to me from my life experiences that He does not force His direction upon me. I must voluntarily submit. If I submitted to Him, He would bless my life and provide both the power and desire to do everything He calls me to do!

Yes, I had received Christ as my Savior when I was eleven years old, but somehow I had missed this life transforming message. I had missed the basis of a powerful relationship with the heavenly Father by the Lord Jesus Christ living out His life through me. Without grasping this truth, I was relegated, as you may be, to a life of failure, frustration and disappointment as a Christian. This truth is fundamental to releasing your CEO within—becoming what God intended for you to be.

There seems to be a pattern in the life of most Christians similar to my experience. Frustration and failure often come in family or business relationships. Confronting the fears of such failure leads to increased self-effort. We work harder, longer and with more intensity. There may come thoughts of escape—change jobs, get a divorce or move to another part of the country. We think that changing our circumstances will lead to fulfillment. After all this effort, the discontent, frustration and failure continue. Life is miserable.

Failure and feelings can begin to break down the wall of pride and push us toward seeking help. Our only Source for solution is the Lord. Openness and transparency before Him leads us to the truth. Through faith we grasp the truth expressed so beautifully in the Scripture: "I am crucified with Christ; it is no longer I who live, but Christ lives in me; and the life which I now live in the flesh I live by faith in the Son of God, who loved me and gave Himself for me." (Galatians 2:20)

A Christian can continue in self-effort and miss this truth until the grave. The title of Hannah Whitehall Smith's classic book, *The Christian Secret of a Happy Life*, gives the answer. It seems to be a secret because so few discover the truth and surrender every aspect of their lives to the Lord. I am so grateful for the beginning of the process on that night so long ago.

The secret was revealed to me and I yielded control of my life to the Lord as I surrendered my rights to Him. The revelation that the Lord had a will and a purpose for my business life as well as my family was a staggering and exciting discovery. It had never occurred to me that He was interested in business. Because of my lack of understanding this truth, I had compartmentalized my life and neatly boxed Him out of the picture.

Did I learn all this in that one message? No, but the seeds of future growth were sown and the platform was laid for my future concept of success. Later I understood even more; He would pour His life out through me as I yielded to Him.

Following that night of revelation and commitment, I knew that I wanted to continue to achieve excellence—doing my best. But there had begun a work in me; I now knew that my best totally depended upon Him and He would be my focus. My new attitude continued to grow; His best through me in the years ahead. Grasping this marvelous truth and the fact that I was now working for the Lord (Colossians 3:22) changed my attitude and I began praying about every decision.

In the months ahead, my whole concept of success was changed and expanded as I thought about the message I had heard. The Lord led me to a quiet confidence in His directing my path; if He wanted me in my particular job, He would bless my work. If He wanted me elsewhere, He would move me to a different job.

"Confidence in the natural world is self-reliance; in the spiritual world it is God-reliance."
—Oswald Chambers

A further understanding became a living reality. As a child I had believed that a spiritual calling was only for ministers or missionaries. I thought other vocations were only necessary in order to make a living. This enlightening led me to see that the Lord had "called" me to the business arena. The knowledge of being "called" to my work, gave me a new sense of purpose. He would provide the desire to do what He called me to do and would give me the power to carry out that purpose. High quality decisions were made. There was a new excitement and enthusiasm for the future. There was a love for my work and a new sensitivity and love toward my fellow workers.

The Lord's intent is to express Himself through Christians not only in life in general, but also in the context of the marketplace. The Lord will use us in the lives of those we serve, which includes all those around us. My new desire was to be available and ready to serve others, customers, employees and their families through my vocation, my calling.

> *"There is no burnout when your work is based on a love relationship!"*
> —*Lloyd John Ogilvie*

The Lord uses failure as a platform for success. Failure itself is not the issue, but how we respond to it. Winston Churchill once defined success as the ability to move from failure to failure without losing your enthusiasm.

Within a few months, the Baton Rouge office became the number one office in the company. I was challenged and contented in this location and in this job. But the Lord did not allow us to stay in this comfort zone. He moved us on to Atlanta, Georgia, where I became general manager for one of the two divisions. As I had been learning to be faithful in little things, now I was being put in charge of bigger things.

My experience with adversity and failure in Baton Rouge led me to the most important aspect of my definition of success. The Lord became the central focus. This new enlightened definition was based on my response to failure and adversity. Someone defined success as "what you have become compared to what you are capable of becoming." I began to think about success as a measure of how much of His purpose was being accomplished in my life. The new definition was essentially based on Psalm 139 which explains that the Lord had a plan for our lives before we were born. Success is what you have become compared to all that the Lord planned for you before you were born. You will notice that there are no definite goals or targets for income in this definition. My income had increased dramatically as a result of our performance, but now I knew and acknowledged that my income was His provision. Finally, I realized that the number of zeros on my W-2 was not the way to measure success.

Just a few years after moving to Atlanta, I became president of the company. Being president of a publicly held company opened up a new world for me. Having my earnings and all company information in the public arena was totally new to me. It was a fishbowl experience and I was one of the fish!

The new position brought all kinds of new thoughts concerning my future. How was a president of a publicly held company supposed to look and act? Should things change? We had wanted a larger home for some time. We wanted more space for our four children and their social activities. Our mothers were growing older and would eventually need our help and perhaps to live with us. We bought a new home in Buckhead, an upscale location in Atlanta. We joined the Cherokee Town and Country Club, a prestigious private club.

My friend and financial counselor, Larry Burkett, and I discussed my purchasing a Mercedes. Larry asked two questions: "Do you plan to pay cash for the car, and will you keep the car 10 years?" With a resounding yes to both questions, Larry's advice was to purchase the Mercedes. He said that it was a good investment under those conditions. I was sure that my friend knew I did not want to take an ego trip with all this new "stuff."

With all the joys of my new position as president, I began to read the proxy statements of other companies. The study revealed something I had not expected. There were many others in similar positions who were being paid substantially more than I was being paid. My newfound significance was being destroyed because of that sneaky thief, comparison.

At church one Sunday right in the middle of my continuing comparison, I heard a message about gratitude. The light of understanding dawned. Comparison breeds discontentment! I recognized and confessed how foolish I was being. The Lord reminded me that I had been blessed far beyond my expectations. My attitude needed to be refocused on gratitude *again*—fostering a grateful spirit for all the blessings that were mine rather than comparing my situation to others'. II Corinthians 10:12, "For we dare not class ourselves or compare ourselves with those who commend themselves. But they, measuring themselves by themselves, and comparing themselves among themselves, are not wise." Yes, I saw my foolishness, yet there was one other critical lesson I learned about making comparisons: God's standard, not the world's standard was to be my only measure.

In the early English versions of the Bible, the word success is only used one time. It's found in Joshua 1:7-8 and provides specific directions for achieving success: "Only you be strong and very courageous, that you may do according to all the law which Moses My servant commanded you. Turn not from it to the right hand or to the left that you may prosper wherever you go. This Book of the Law shall not depart out of your mouth, but you shall meditate on it day and night, that you may observe to do according to all that is written in it. For then you shall make your way prosperous, and then you shall deal wisely and have good success." (Joshua 1:8-9 AMP) The Lord promises success and prosperity to those who know His Word, internalize it, and obey it. In the process of knowing and internalizing His Word, it becomes the first consideration in every situation. God's will literally will become our will and we should not hesitate to step out in obedience. We are habitually "all out" for God. There is no doubt that this is the Lord's plan and embodies his definition of success.

At Rotary Club, a eulogy was given for one of our members. His wife and family were present, and the eulogy was given by one of the older members who knew the deceased quite well. The speaker summarized his friend's life with an explanation of why our fellow Rotarian was such a good man. He loved God above everything and anything else. He believed God was the Author of the Bible and therefore it was Truth. He believed every word and lived by it. What a tribute and a picture of true success!

This reminded me of a T-shirt I saw at the beach. Printed in bold letters, it read: "There is a God, and it is not you!" This is a wonderful thought to keep in the top of your mind since we live in a world occupied by massive egos, mine having been one of them. We must remember the truth of Psalm 100:3: "It is He who has made us, and not we ourselves."

As I continued my journey in the marketplace, I studied the Scriptures and discovered several verses that had a profound impact on my destination. We each determine our own priorities, and the Bible makes it clear how we should prioritize our lives. Matthew 6:33 serves as a moment-by-moment reminder of exactly where my focus should be in seeking His plan for my destination: "He will give you all you need from day to day if you live for him and make the Kingdom of God your primary concern." (NLT) My focus must FIRST be upon Him.

There is also the danger of being double-minded. "A double-minded man [is] unstable in all his ways." (James 1:8) I was double-minded when I became confused about my priorities—I was hesitating, irresolute, and dubious. My struggle came when I wavered in my commitment and focus, trying to serve God and money. Through the process of change in my thinking regarding money, the Scripture regarding the love of money became a battlefield where I fought repeated challenges. This verse made many issues I faced incredibly clear: "For what profit is it to a man if he gains the whole world, and is himself destroyed or lost?" (Luke 9:25)

The following Scripture from Proverbs became a platform for all decisions, not only in my life but for our entire company: "Choose a good reputation over great riches, for being held in high esteem is better than having silver or gold." (Proverbs 22:1 NLT)

The more Scripture verses I internalized, the more the Lord refined my definition of success. For me, the motive of giving and serving came into play strongly as the proper measure of success. Luke 6:38 promises: "If you give, you will receive. Your gift will return to you in full measure, pressed down, shaken together to make room for more, and running over. Whatever measure you use in giving—large or small—it will be used to measure what is given back to you." (NLT)

I am confident that you are reading this book because you want to be a success. Don't be limited by an improper concept of success as I was earlier in my career. My concept of success developed over a period of time. I would encourage you to develop an accurate concept from God's perspective today!

To determine your destination, you will have to examine yourself, your motives, and your basic beliefs and filter them through the Lord's standard. Your definition will become the basic foundation and framework of all your thought processes; otherwise, you'll be distracted by the world. To formulate your definition by God's standard is not the normal or natural thing in business today. If you tell your associates, they most likely will not believe you, and they may even laugh at you. They will only believe it when they see it in your actions.

> *"Success is not final, failure is not fatal: It is the courage to*
> *continue that counts."*
> —*Winston Churchill*

As a Christian, I have potential far beyond what I ever thought or imagined. The reality of the Holy Spirit dwelling in me changed my entire perspective. I had a new measuring stick for everyday experiences.

My wife wrote a definition of success in her first book, *Her Husband is Known in the Gates*, that best expresses my thoughts. She says success is "when one is engaged in work which gives him satisfaction and a sense of significance, has a good name and reputation, has a rich personal relationship with his wife and family, and is habitually all out for God." This definition framed much of my career and the way I viewed each new opportunity. Formulating your definition of success is critical. Only when you know your destination will you know when you arrive!

> *"God does have a plan for success, and, although it's unique for*
> *each individual, it is common in three ways:*
> *God never provides success at the expense of serving Him first.*
> *God never provides success at the expense of our peace.*
> *God never provides success at the expense of the family."*
> —*Larry Burkett*

When you focus on these principles and apply them to your own experience, it will be easier to determine your destination. Learn

God's perspective from His Word, internalize it, and personalize your definition. Include these Biblical concepts as you adopt your own definition:

- Success is Godly character and spiritual fruit! Knowing and obeying God's Word is a requirement for success.

- Understanding your unique calling in life must be a part of your definition. There is great freedom in working for the Lord in the power of the Holy Spirit.

- Trust the Lord for all promotions; work hard; commit to excellence in all your work as for Him. Use the Lord's ways, not political or manipulative methods. Wait on the Lord!

- The Lord has given you special talents and knowledge, and He prepared tasks specifically for you. "We are His workmanship, created in Christ Jesus for good works, which God prepared beforehand that we should walk in them." (Ephesians 2:10)

- Be constantly aware that there is no success if you wreck your family while pursuing it. To succeed in one and fail in the other is no success!

"It is not your business to succeed, but to do right; when you have done so, the rest lies with God."
—C. S. Lewis

Success is an elusive moving target in the secular world. It is a frustrating experience to pursue it. God's perspective presents a totally different concept. The fulfillment is unique for each individual. God has a plan for you! He provides the desire and power to achieve. Otherwise we are just fallen creatures seeking for something better. When you submit your life to Him and discover His plan for you, the release of your CEO within will become a reality!

Conclusion

The now familiar feeling of awe wells up in me as I sit in the Supreme Court. The building itself demands respect. It is a picture of true dignity, patriotism, and respect for the laws of our country. It is certainly in keeping with the importance and dignity of the Court and Judiciary as a coequal independent branch of the Federal government. Many images on the walls of the structure capture my attention. The great lawgivers are depicted, and my favorite is the Old Testament figure, Moses.

My focus is fixed—I'm watching and listening as Associate Justice Clarence Thomas places medallions around the necks of the newly inducted members of the Horatio Alger Association of Distinguished Americans. I revisit this impressive scene every year, now as a spectator. Without intention, I find my thoughts straying back to my treasured memory of my own induction in 2001.

Well-known men and women such as Billy Graham, Oprah Winfrey, Ronald Reagan, Jack Kemp, Truett Cathy, Mary Higgins Clark, and Roger Staubach have received this honor. Then there are those who are not so well-known—like me. Every member has a true "Horatio Alger" story—from rags to riches. Each inductee has an amazing history of overcoming unbelievable odds and hardships in order to release the CEO within!

Many people achieve what seems to spectators like great success, prestige, power, and prosperity in life, yet there is a great difference for the Christian. The Christian man or woman who has a heart for the Lord depends upon an entirely different Source for achievement and releasing the CEO within. This Source works for any individual—the homemaker, the repairman, the president, the chairman of a large company. A computer also works for anyone, but there is tremendous power available to the user when it's connected to the Internet. That power only becomes available by getting connected. The same thing is true of the principles I have shared in this book. The full release of the CEO within is based on a relationship, not a religion. We get connected through relationship.

A high-ranking man in the field of religion came to Jesus at night so that no one would see him. We might view him today as a bishop, cardinal, or president of a denomination, a man known for his religious conviction and position. Nicodemus addressed Jesus as being from God because of the miracles he had witnessed. Jesus responded, "Unless you are born again, you cannot see the kingdom of God." Nicodemus wanted to know what Jesus meant. Jesus explained that when we are born, we are born of the flesh. In order to have a relationship with Him, we must have a spiritual birth. Without the spiritual birth, no one will ever see the kingdom of God. That spiritual birth takes place when we believe in and receive Jesus as our personal Savior. Jesus explained to Nicodemus:

> *"For God so loved the world that He gave His only begotten Son,*
> *that whoever believes in Him should not perish*
> *but have everlasting life.*
> *For God did not send His Son into the world to condemn the world,*
> *but that the world through Him might be saved." (John 3:16-17)*

Believing is a matter of faith. We put our trust in Jesus. We cling to and rely on Him. When we come to the realization that we are sinful and separated from God, we then can see that trusting Jesus is the only answer to the dilemma—being separated from God.

> *"Faith cannot be intellectually defined. It's the inborn ability*
> *to see God in everything."*
> *—Oswald Chambers*

As we see clearly from Nicodemus' story, religion is not the answer to man's dilemma. The only answer is to get connected to Jesus by receiving Him into our lives and experiencing the change and new life He offers each of us. The Lord provides both the desire and the power to do all things in His plan, including everything shared in this book.

The new birth provides the basis for establishing your own unique calling and purpose in life. As you internalize Biblical concepts of success, wealth, and God's work in and through you, your entire life will be revitalized and the purpose for which you were created will be released. This is, in fact, the Christian's secret of releasing the CEO within.

> *"The call of God is like the call of the sea. No one hears it but the one who has the nature of the sea in him."*
> —*Oswald Chambers*

Other books by Wes and Bernadine Cantrell

High Performance Ethics
Wes Cantrell and Jim Lucas
Published by Tyndale House

Her Husband is Known in the Gates
Bending the Twig
By Bernadine Cantrell

Contact Information
wesc1@bellsouth.net
http://www.bernadineandwes.blogspot.com

LaVergne, TN USA
10 January 2010
169481LV00003B/2/P